IFIP Advances in Information and Communication Technology

624

Editor-in-Chief

Kai Rannenberg, Goethe University Frankfurt, Germany

Editorial Board Members

IFIP – The International Federation for Information Processing

IFIP was founded in 1960 under the auspices of UNESCO, following the first World Computer Congress held in Paris the previous year. A federation for societies working in information processing, IFIP's aim is two-fold: to support information processing in the countries of its members and to encourage technology transfer to developing nations. As its mission statement clearly states:

> IFIP is the global non-profit federation of societies of ICT professionals that aims at achieving a worldwide professional and socially responsible development and application of information and communication technologies.

IFIP is a non-profit-making organization, run almost solely by 2500 volunteers. It operates through a number of technical committees and working groups, which organize events and publications. IFIP's events range from large international open conferences to working conferences and local seminars.

The flagship event is the IFIP World Computer Congress, at which both invited and contributed papers are presented. Contributed papers are rigorously refereed and the rejection rate is high.

As with the Congress, participation in the open conferences is open to all and papers may be invited or submitted. Again, submitted papers are stringently refereed.

The working conferences are structured differently. They are usually run by a working group and attendance is generally smaller and occasionally by invitation only. Their purpose is to create an atmosphere conducive to innovation and development. Refereeing is also rigorous and papers are subjected to extensive group discussion.

Publications arising from IFIP events vary. The papers presented at the IFIP World Computer Congress and at open conferences are published as conference proceedings, while the results of the working conferences are often published as collections of selected and edited papers.

IFIP distinguishes three types of institutional membership: Country Representative Members, Members at Large, and Associate Members. The type of organization that can apply for membership is a wide variety and includes national or international societies of individual computer scientists/ICT professionals, associations or federations of such societies, government institutions/government related organizations, national or international research institutes or consortia, universities, academies of sciences, companies, national or international associations or federations of companies.

More information about this series at http://www.springer.com/series/6102

Davide Taibi · Valentina Lenarduzzi ·
Terhi Kilamo · Stefano Zacchiroli (Eds.)

Open Source Systems

17th IFIP WG 2.13 International Conference, OSS 2021
Virtual Event, May 12–13, 2021
Proceedings

 Springer

Editors
Davide Taibi (iD)
Tampere University
Tampere, Finland

Valentina Lenarduzzi (iD)
LUT University
Lahti, Finland

Terhi Kilamo (iD)
Tampere University
Tampere, Finland

Stefano Zacchiroli (iD)
Université de Paris and Inria
Paris, France

ISSN 1868-4238   ISSN 1868-422X (electronic)
IFIP Advances in Information and Communication Technology
ISBN 978-3-030-75250-7   ISBN 978-3-030-75251-4 (eBook)
https://doi.org/10.1007/978-3-030-75251-4

This Springer imprint is published by the registered company Springer Nature Switzerland AG
The registered company address is: Gewerbestrasse 11, 6330 Cham, Switzerland

Preface

This book constitutes the refereed proceedings of the 17th IFIP WG 2.13 International Conference on Open Source Systems, OSS 2021, held in Lahti, Finland, during May 12–13, 2021. Due to the COVID-19 pandemic, the conference was held virtually.

The 6 revised full papers and 1 short paper presented were carefully reviewed and selected from 23 submissions (a 30.4% acceptance rate). All of the submitted research papers went through a rigorous peer-review process. Each paper was reviewed by at least two members of the Program Committee.

The papers cover a wide range of topics in the field of free/libre open source software (FLOSS) and discuss theories, practices, experiences, and tools relating to the development and applications of FLOSS systems. There is a specific focus on two aspects: the development of open source systems and the underlying technical, social, and economic issues; and the adoption of FLOSS solutions and the implications of such adoption, both in the public and in the private sector.

We hope that you find the OSS 2021 proceedings useful for your professional and academic activities, and that you enjoyed the conference. Finally, we would like to thank all the people who have contributed to OSS 2021 including the authors, the sponsors, the reviewers, the volunteers, and the chairs.

March 2021

Davide Taibi
Valentina Lenarduzzi
Terhi Kilamo
Stefano Zacchiroli

Organization

Organizing Committee

General Chair

Davide Taibi — Tampere University, Finland

Program Co-chairs

Valentina Lenarduzzi — LUT University, Finland
Stefano Zacchiroli — Université de Paris and Inria, France

Special Issue Chair

Fabio Palomba — University of Salerno, Italy

Proceedings Chair

Terhi Kilamo — Tampere University, Finland

Publicity Chair

Gemma Catolino — Tilburg University and Jheronimus Academy of Data Science, Netherlands

Local Co-chairs

Sami Hyrynsalmi — LUT University, Finland
Sonja Hyrynsalmi — LUT University, Finland

Virtualization Co-chairs

Antti Knutas — LUT University, Finland
Francesco Lomio — Tampere University, Finland
Savanna Lujan — Tampere University, Finland
Sergio Moreschini — Tampere University, Finland

Web Chair

José Carlos Camposano — LUT University, Finland

Program Committee

Valentina Lenarduzzi — LUT University, Finland
Stefano Zacchiroli — Université de Paris and Inria, France
Alexandre Decan — University of Mons, Belgium

Ann Barcomb   Friedrich-Alexander University Erlangen-Nürnberg,
                                         Germany / Lero - The Irish Software Research
                                         Centre and University of Limerick, Ireland
Moritz Beller   Facebook, USA
Fabio Calefato   University of Bari, Italy
Andrea Capiluppi   Brunel University London, UK
Paolo Ciancarini   University of Bologna, Italy / Innopolis University,
                                         Russia
Kevin Crowston   Syracuse University, USA
Javier Luis Cánovas   IN3-UOC, Spain
    Izquierdo
Tapajit Dey   Lero - The Irish Software Research Centre and
                                         University of Limerick, Ireland
Davide Di Ruscio   University of L'Aquila, Italy
Dirk Riehle   Friedrich-Alexander University Erlangen-Nürnberg,
                                         Germany
Stefane Fermigier   Abilian SAS, France
Christina von Flach Garcia   Federal University of Bahia, Brazil
    Chavez
Jesus M.   Universidad Rey Juan Carlos, Spain
    Gonzalez-Barahona
Akinori Ihara   Wakayama University, Japan
Daniel Izquierdo Cortazat   Bitergia, Spain
Daniel S. Katz   University of Illinois at Urbana-Champaign, USA
Luigi Lavazza   Università degli Studi dell'Insubria, Italy
Panos Louridas   Athens University of Economics and Business, Greece
Björn Lundell   University of Skövde, Sweden
Manuel Mazzara   Innopolis University, Russia
Paulo Meirelles   University of São Paulo, Brazil
Sandro Morasca   Università degli Studi dell'Insubria, Italy
Tetsuo Noda   Shimane University, Japan
Lucas Nussbaum   University of Lorraine, France
Antoine Pietri   Inria, France
Peter Rigby   Concordia University, Canada
Gregorio Robles   Universidad Rey Juan Carlos, Spain
Alberto Sillitti   Innopolis University, Russia
Diomidis Spinellis   Athens University of Economics and Business, Greece
Igor Steinmacher   Universidade Tecnológica Federal do Paraná, Brazil
Anthony I. (Tony)   Carnegie Mellon, Silicon Valley, USA
    Wasserman

Contents

Contents

Comparing Static Analysis and Code Smells as Defect Predictors: An Empirical Study

Luigi Lavazza[1]($\boxtimes$)(ID), Sandro Morasca[1,2](ID), and Davide Tosi[1](ID)

[1] Università degli Studi dell'Insubria, Varese, Italy
{luigi.lavazza,davide.tosi}@uninsubria.it
[2] Università degli Studi dell'Insubria, Como, Italy
sandro.morasca@uninsubria.it

Abstract. *Background.* Industrial software increasingly relies on open source software. Therefore, industrial practitioners need to evaluate the quality of a specific open source product they are considering for adoption. Automated tools greatly help assess open source software quality, by reducing the related costs, but do not provide perfectly reliable indications. Indications from tools can be used to restrict and focus manual code inspections, which are typically expensive and time-consuming, only on the code sections most likely to contain faults. *Aim.* We investigate the extent of the effectiveness of static analysis bug detectors by themselves and in combination with code smell detectors in guiding inspections. *Method.* We performed an empirical study, in which we used a bug detector (SpotBugs) and a code smell detector (JDeodorant). *Results.* Our results show that the selected bug detector is precise enough to justify inspecting the code it flags as possibly buggy. Applying the considered code smell detector makes predictions even more precise, but at the price of a rather low recall. *Conclusions.* Using the considered tools as inspection drivers proved quite useful. The relatively small size of our study does not allow us to draw universally valid conclusions, but our results should be applicable to source code of any kind, although they were obtained from open source code.

Keywords: Defect prediction · Code smell · Static analysis

1 Introduction

Software inspections [5,6,12,13] are one of the main techniques that have been proposed for discovering defects in code, to prevent defective software from being released. Software inspections are often performed with the help of checklists, i.e., lists of recurrent issues that usually lead to software failure.

Software bug detectors based on static analysis were developed to automatically recognize code patterns that are generally associated with defects.

© IFIP International Federation for Information Processing 2021
Published by Springer Nature Switzerland AG 2021
D. Taibi et al. (Eds.): OSS 2021, IFIP AICT 624, pp. 1–15, 2021.
https://doi.org/10.1007/978-3-030-75251-4_1

Bug detectors perform a sort of "automated" inspection, as opposed to the "manual" inspection performed by developers. Unfortunately, static analysis cannot in general provide conclusive evidence of defects. Since many properties related to software defects are undecidable, the indications provided by bug detectors must be verified by developers. In practice, developers have to manually inspect the portions of code that are flagged as possibly defective by tools. Because of their high cost, manual inspections are usually performed only on the sections of code that are considered particularly important or very error-prone. In this sense, bug detectors may be very effective, since they indicate which parts of the code are worth inspecting manually.

The concept of "code smell" was introduced to describe a code structure that is likely to cause problems [8,16,36]. The original introduction of the concept of code smell was based on the manual examination of the source code, as witnessed by a few indications. First, Fowler et al. [16] provided only informal descriptions of code smells, since code smells are expected to be easily recognized as inadequate code structures by professional software coders. Second, they did not intend to provide any precise measurement-based definition of code smells (*"In our experience no set of metrics rivals informed human intuition"* [16]). Third, no additional evidence was required that code smells actually have detrimental effects on software. The very same act of code analysis by which a developer recognizes a code smell also lets him/her recognize its harmfulness, hence a situation that is not deemed dangerous is not classified as a code smell, even when the code structurally matches the definition of a code smell.

However, manual code smell detection involves the same type of costs as manual inspections. Therefore, to reduce development costs [23], researchers have developed tools for automatically detecting code smells [9,28,29,43,44,50]. Automation was made possible by precise definitions of code smells, generally based on static measures of source code [27].

Even though automatic code smell detectors have been available for a few years, there is little evidence that automatically detected code smells are actually associated with quality issues: there are both reports that support and do not support the association of the presence of code smells with software quality issues. For instance, Olbrich et al. [30] and Palomba et al. [31] reported findings supporting the hypothesis that god class hinders maintainability, while Schumacher et al. [38], Sjøberg et al. [40] and Yamashita et al. [48] reported findings not supporting the hypothesis. Some articles even report cases in which an improvement of software quality in presence of code smells was observed [17].

Other papers studied the correlation between code smells and some structural problems reported by FindBugs, without checking manually whether the detected structural problems correspond to actual defects [11,41,51]. In our view, code sections that are classified as smelly by automated detectors should be considered as code sections that need to be manually inspected, to check whether the conditions that could hamper software quality are satisfied.

Given that bug detectors have proved to work reasonably well in detecting real bugs [24,45,52], and that manual inspections are expensive, it would be important for software developers to know how well automated bug detectors work by themselves and in combination with code smell detectors. In fact, practitioners who have a given budget for inspections must decide how they should spend it most effectively. Should they favor the indications by bug detectors? Should they inspect the code flagged by automated smell detectors? Or maybe should they proceed to modify the code without inspecting it at all, based exclusively on the indications by the tools? In this paper, we address these questions by investigating the extent of the effectiveness of static analysis as bugs detector by itself and in combination with code smells in guiding inspections. These questions are important especially when developers reuse software written by other developers, as is usually the case with Open Source Software (OSS) [25, 26].

We illustrate an empirical study concerning the OSS products incorporated in two B2C web portals developed by an industrial organization. Our study provides some early findings on the effectiveness of bug detectors aiming at problem detection and automated code smell detection tools. Specifically, we used one tool per category: respectively, SpotBugs [4] and JDeodorant [2]. We applied them to the set of OSS products incorporated in two B2C web portals. We first applied SpotBugs and noted the subset of most important warnings that it issued. We then proceeded to manually check whether those warnings corresponded to actual bugs. Finally, we subjected the code sections related to the warnings to JDeodorant and recorded the smells found.

The main contributions of the paper are the following:

- Given the constant evolution of tools, our study provides some up-to-date evidence about their practical usefulness in software development.
- In our empirical study, we found that the *precision* of the tools in detecting problematic code sections is reasonably high, despite the fact that they do not consider the dynamic behavior of the software under analysis.
- For the first time—to the best of our knowledge—a quantitative evaluation of using bug detectors in combination with code smell detectors is provided.
- We provide some quantitative performance indicators to developers who need to decide how to evaluate the quality of the OSS they are using, or could use, as part of their software.

The results presented in this paper were obtained by applying a process that is close to the one used by practitioners. So, our results are expected to be directly applicable in software development practice.

The remainder of the paper is organized as follows. Section 2 describes the concepts, processes and tools that are the subject of the study. Section 3 describes our empirical study and illustrates the results we obtained. Section 4 discusses the threats to the validity of the study. Section 5 reports about the previous work that aimed at evaluating bug detectors based on static analysis and code smells. Section 6 draws some conclusions.

2   Bug Detectors and Code Smell Detectors

Several tools exist that can be used to reduce inspection costs.

We used two static analysis tools in our empirical study: SpotBugs to automatically detect potential bugs in a software program, and JDeodorant to detect potential code smells and suggest refactoring strategies to improve the source code. These tools were selected because of their characteristics and their diffusion in research and practice. Both tools have very active communities. Both tools are also available as plug-ins, such as for Eclipse or SonarQube platforms.

2.1   A Bug Detector: SpotBugs

SpotBugs [4] is a static analysis tool that looks for bugs in Java source code. The tool is free software, distributed under the GNU Lesser General Public License. SpotBugs inherits all of the features of its predecessor FindBugs [1, 19] and checks more than 400 bug patterns. SpotBugs checks for bug patterns such as—among others—null pointer dereferencing, infinite recursive loops, bad uses of the Java libraries, and deadlocks. SpotBugs is available as an Eclipse plugin at [spotbugs.github.io/eclipse/] or as a standalone program and can be downloaded from [spotbugs.github.io].

In SpotBugs, bug patterns are classified by means of several variables, such as: the type of violation, its category, the rank of the bug, and the confidence of the discovering process.

Ten categories are defined [3], such as "Bad Practice" (i.e., violations of recommended and essential coding practice, like hash code and equals problems, cloneable idiom, dropped exceptions, Serializable problems, and misuse of finalize), "Correctness" (i.e., probable bug - an apparent coding mistake resulting in code that was probably not what the developer intended), or "Multithreaded correctness" (i.e., code flaw issues having to do with threads, locks, and volatiles). The complete list of bug descriptions can be found at [spotbugs.readthedocs.io/en/latest/bugDescriptions.html].

The rank of each warning concerns the severity of the potential bug, and spans from 1 (most severe) to 20 (least severe). Four rank levels are also defined: "scariest" ($1 \leq rank \leq 4$), "scary" ($5 \leq rank \leq 9$), "worrying" ($10 \leq rank \leq 14$), "of concern" ($15 \leq rank \leq 20$).

Moreover, a "confidence" (named "priority" in earlier releases of SpotBugs) is associated to each warning: high confidence (1), normal confidence (2) and low confidence (3), to highlight the quality of the detection process.

2.2   A Code Smells Detector: JDeodorant

JDeodorant [2, 15, 42] is a free tool (available as an Eclipse plug-in) that detects design problems in source code, such as code smells, and suggests how to resolve these smells by applying refactoring procedures. Specifically, JDeodorant is able to detect the following four code smells [16]: God Class (a class that is too long, too complex, and does too much), Long Method (a method, function or procedure that is too large), Type Checking (a class contains "complicated conditional statements that make the code difficult to understand and maintain" [14]), and Feature Envy (a method or an object does not leverage data or methods from its class but asks for external data or methods to perform computation or make a decision).

3   The Empirical Study

3.1   Method

Recently, one of the authors participated in the analysis of the quality of an industrial software product, which used several pieces of OSS [22]. In this study we use those OSS programs, briefly described in Table 1, as a test bed. In practice, the quality of a large fraction of industrial software depends on the quality of OSS. By selecting a set of OSS products that we know are used also in non open-source contexts, we make sure to 1) analyze software that is relevant, and 2) provide results that are of interest also outside the OSS community.

Table 1. The open-source products that were analyzed.

Product name	Version	LOC	Num classes	Num methods
Log4j	1.2.16	16497	217	1910
Jasperreports	6.11.0	278694	2558	23465
Pdfbox	1.8.16	120037	1125	9164
Hibernate-search-elasticsearch	5.11.4	21575	350	3264
Hibernate-search-backend-jgroups	5.11.4	1624	25	1067
Hibernate-search-engine	5.11.4	65239	1020	7967
Hibernate-search-performance-orm	5.11.4	1950	39	159

The study was organized in three phases: data extraction, data analysis, and interpretation of results.

Data extraction was performed as follows:

1. We applied SpotBugs to the set of OSS products. SpotBugs issued several hundred warnings. To limit the effort needed to inspect the code flagged as possibly defective, we considered only the 64 issues having rank not greater than 11. Since SpotBugs ranks warning severity in the range 1–20, we chose 11 as a threshold since it is the upper median of the severity rank range. Considering the issues with the highest ranks is just what developers would do in an industrial setting: having a limited effort to be dedicated to inspections, they deal with the issues classified as most dangerous.

2. The considered issues reported by SpotBugs were inspected manually by the authors. The inspections resulted in classifying every issue as either confirmed (when a real defect was found), rejected (when a false positive was recognized), or "possible" (when we found something wrong, but our knowledge of the code did not allow us to decide whether a failure was actually bound to occur).
3. The code elements (i.e., the classes or methods) involved in the issues reported by SpotBugs were analyzed with JDeodorant, and the detected smells were annotated. We focused on performing smell detection on elements already flagged defective by SpotBugs since, in this paper, we are interested in evaluating the effectiveness of static analysis bug detectors by themselves and in combination with code smell detectors in guiding inspections, and not *vice versa*.

For instance, in our study, SpotBugs issued a warning of category Correctness and type `rc_ref_comparison` (which is issued when `==` or `!=` operators were used instead of `equals()`) in method `validateEqualWithDefault` of class `Elasticsearch2SchemaValidator`, package `hibernate.search.elasticsearch`. JDeodorant highlighted that class `Elasticsearch2SchemaValidator` is a smelly class (God Class), and method `validateEqualWithDefault` suffers from Feature Envy. Moreover, manual inspection confirmed that the SpotBugs warning is associated with a real bug.

Data analysis was conducted on the set of code elements flagged as defective by SpotBugs. The analysis was performed twice: once considering the "possible" bugs as false positives, and once considering the "possible" bugs as true positives. In what follows, we label the former scenario as "optimistic" (since the code is less buggy than indicated by SpotBugs), and the latter scenario as "pessimistic" (since the code is considered as buggy as indicated by SpotBugs).

Data analysis was conducted as follows (once for each scenario). First, we computed the number of true positive (TP), false positive (FP), true negative (TN), and false negative (FN) estimates provided by SpotBugs and JDeodorant for both scenarios (see Table 3). In doing this, the existence of a given smell was considered as a fault prediction.

Then, based on TP, FP, TN and FN, we computed a few accuracy indicators, namely *precision, recall, F-measure* (the harmonic mean of *precision* and *recall*), and ϕ, alias Matthews' Correlation Coefficient (MCC):

$$precision = \frac{TP}{EP} = \frac{TP}{TP+FP}$$

$$recall = \frac{TP}{AP} = \frac{TP}{TP+FN}$$

$$F\text{-}measure = \frac{2\ precision\ recall}{precision+recall}$$

$$\phi = \frac{TP\ TN - FP\ FN}{\sqrt{EP\ EN\ AP\ AN}}$$

where EP is the number of estimated positives (EP = TP+FP), EN is the number of estimated negatives (EN = TN+FN), AP is the number of actual positives (AP = TP+FN) and AN is the number of actual negatives (AN = TN+FP).

Finally, we considered two additional smell-based faultiness predictions, which we labeled "any smell" and "all smells." In the former case, a code element is estimated buggy if it has one or more of the smells detected by JDeodorant; in the latter case, a code element is estimated buggy if it has all of the smells detected by JDeodorant. We computed the same accuracy indicators mentioned above for "any smell" and "all smells."

3.2 Results

First of all, let us evaluate the performance of SpotBugs. We considered 64 warnings, hence EP = 64. Among these, in the optimistic scenario, TP is the number of confirmed bugs; in the pessimistic scenario, TP is the number of confirmed and possible bugs. Note that we consider only warnings, which—according to SpotBugs—concern potential problems, hence there are estimated positives, but no estimated negatives. Thus, EP = 64 = n, where n indicates the total number of estimates of the classifier implemented by SpotBugs. As a consequence, we have TN = FN = 0, hence TP = AP, and *recall* = 1.

The first row of Table 2 summarizes the performance of SpotBugs. Specifically, SpotBugs issued 64 warnings; of these, 37 were recognized via inspections as real bugs, 13 were recognized as false positives, while 14 could not be classified with certainty. Accordingly, in the optimistic case (i.e., when possible bugs are considered as false positives) $precision = \frac{37}{64} \simeq 0.54$. In the pessimistic case (i.e., when possible bugs are considered as true positives) $precision = \frac{37+14}{64} \simeq 0.8$.

The first row of Table 2 shows that the accuracy of SpotBugs's predictions is good, substantially better than reported in several previous studies (for instance, Shen et al. reported in their study that FindBugs achieved *precision* = 40% [39]).

Table 2. SpotBug's issues and *precision*.

Selected issues	n	Bugs			*precision*	
		Confirmed	Possible	Rejected	Optimistic	Pessimistic
All	64	37	14	13	0.58	0.80
High rank	6	6	0	0	1.00	1.00
Mid rank	36	13	11	12	0.36	0.67
Low rank	22	18	3	1	0.82	0.95
High conf.	22	10	7	5	0.45	0.77
Mid conf.	42	27	7	8	0.64	0.81

To verify the reliability of the evaluation of the confidence in the warnings, we split SpotBugs issues into high- and mid-confidence ones (there were no low-confidence issues among the ones we considered). We also split SpotBugs issues into high-, mid- and low-rank ones (corresponding to SpotBugs "scariest," "scary," and "worrying" rank levels), to check if the estimation accuracy depends on the rank. The results we obtained are in Table 2. The only noticeable result is that all the 6 high-rank reported issues concern real bugs.

The accuracy indicators for SpotBugs and the considered code smells evaluated by JDeodorant for the optimistic and pessimistic case are given in Table 3. Note that ϕ is undefined for SpotBugs: this is a consequence of EN being zero.

3.3   Interpretation of Results

In interpreting the results, we must take into consideration a few facts:

- For SpotBugs, n = EP, hence FN = TN = 0: thus $recall = \frac{TP}{AP} = \frac{TP}{TP+FN} = \frac{TP}{TP} = 1$.
- When performing a completely random estimation, you get $precision = recall = F\text{-}measure = \frac{AP}{n}$. Therefore, a prediction model having $F\text{-}measure < \frac{AP}{n}$ should be discarded, since it performs worse than random estimation. In the pessimistic case it is $\frac{AP}{n} = 0.8$, while in the optimistic case it is $\frac{AP}{n} = 0.58$. Better than random values of $F\text{-}measure$ are in bold in Tables 3.

Table 3. Accuracy indicators with the optimistic (AP/n = 0.58) and pessimistic criterion (AP/n = 0.8).

Criterion		TP	FP	FN	TN	recall	precision	FM	ϕ
Optimistic	SpotBugs	37	27	0	0	1.00	0.58	**0.73**	—
	GodClass	15	5	22	22	0.41	0.75	0.53	0.23
	LongMethod	22	5	15	22	0.59	0.81	**0.69**	0.41
	FeatureEnvy	5	1	32	26	0.14	0.83	0.23	0.17
	TypeChecking	9	0	28	27	0.24	1.00	0.39	0.35
	AllSmells	2	0	35	27	0.05	1.00	0.10	0.15
	AnySmell	29	9	8	18	0.78	0.76	**0.77**	0.45
Pessimistic	SpotBugs	51	13	0	0	1.00	0.80	**0.89**	—
	GodClass	18	2	33	11	0.35	0.90	0.51	0.17
	LongMethod	24	3	27	10	0.47	0.89	0.62	0.20
	FeatureEnvy	6	0	45	13	0.12	1.00	0.21	0.16
	TypeChecking	9	0	42	13	0.18	1.00	0.30	0.20
	AllSmells	2	0	49	13	0.04	1.00	0.08	0.09
	AnySmell	34	4	17	9	0.67	0.89	0.76	0.29

- *The F-measure* has been widely criticized in the literature [18, 34, 49], mainly because it does not account for true negatives. In our case, though, this is not a reason not to use the *F-measure* to evaluate SpotBugs, because TN = 0 by construction. As far as code smells are concerned, ϕ complements the *F-measure* in providing a reliable indication of prediction accuracy.

In the pessimistic scenario, no code smell has *F-measure* better than random. The low values of ϕ confirm that in this case code smells are poor defect predictors. However, in the optimistic scenario, Long Method and AnySmell have a *F-measure* better than random, and ϕ confirms that in this case these smells are acceptably good defect predictors. In fact, values of ϕ greater than 0.4 indicate that the association between the defect prediction and model and actual defectiveness is between medium and strong [10].

Nonetheless, in both scenarios, all code smells' *precision* is better than random, and often really good. This is not surprising. Most smells address very specific conditions, which do not occur very frequently. Therefore, they are bound to feature rather low *recall*. On the contrary, when a very specific smell is present, it is expected that there is "something wrong" and a defect is likely present as well. For instance, in the pessimistic scenario, Feature Envy is detected in only 6 cases out of 64, and all 6 code elements were found defective.

3.4 Discussion

SpotBugs appears much more precise than reported by previous—possibly outdated—studies. *Precision* in the [0.58, 0.80] range (depending on "possible" bugs being real bugs or not) suggests that manual inspection of the issues reported by SpotBugs is generally cost-effective. To this end, it is worth noting that SpotBugs describes and localizes possible bugs very precisely. Thus, examining a few lines of code is generally sufficient to recognize the presence of the bug. In many cases, the required correction is also straightforward. So, a first outcome of our analysis is that using SpotBugs to identify the code to be inspected appears cost-effective, even when the evaluated code is OSS, on which industrial developers do not want to invest much effort and time.

However, a practitioner that applied SpotBugs and obtained a set of warnings could still wonder whether SpotBugs warnings are reliable enough to deserve inspections. To clear this doubt, a practitioner could decide to run JDeodorant on the code flagged as possibly defective by SpotBugs, to get further confirmations. Our analyses show (see rows "AnySmell" in Table 3) that this process, which connects static analysis and code smell detection, achieves better *precision* than static analysis by itself, i.e., a greater proportion of inspections find real defects; in other words, inspections are most cost-effective. At the same time, *recall* decreases with respect to inspecting all the warnings issued by SpotBugs; hence, fewer defects are removed.

In conclusion, based on the results of our study, we can suggest that manual code inspection be done following the indications provided by SpotBugs, because its relatively high *precision* level makes it possible to identify (and often correct) several bugs with little effort. However, practitioners may prefer to inspect only code that is flagged as defective by both SpotBugs and JDeodorant; however practitioners are warned that this practice seems to have a slightly increased *precision* and a more substantially decreased *recall*.

Code smells appear characterized by good *precision*. Hence it appears useful to inspect code elements that are classified as smelly. Nonetheless, each inspection could be relatively expensive: for instance, inspecting a God Class involves examining several hundred lines of code. Instead, performing smell detection on elements already flagged defective by bug detectors leads to both increasing the confidence that a smelly piece of code is really defective, and greatly simplifies inspections: in case of a God Class, one does not need to examine the entire class, but only the piece of code flagged defective by the bug detector.

4   Threats to Validity

The external validity of our study may be influenced by the fact that we used only two tools, one for each type of analysis. However, the two tools are among the best-known and most used ones, by both researchers and practitioners. At any rate, we were able to investigate only a few code smells, i.e., all those supported by JDeodorant. So, we may have obtained different results if we had investigated other code smells. Also, we used a limited number of projects and datasets, which may not be representative of a wider section of the software products. In addition, we used OSS projects, which may not be representative of proprietary software products and processes. We limited the number of issues investigated to 64, though we addressed the most critical of a few hundred warnings. As already noted in Sect. 3.1, we performed smell detection only on elements already flagged defective by SpotBugs, because our goal was not to compare the performance of the two tools in isolation. This is a limitation to the scope of the study, not to its validity; readers are warned not to interpret our results as an evaluation of the performance of code smellers when not used in combination with bug detectors.

Construct validity may be threatened by the performance metrics used. For instance, *FM* has been widely used in the literature, but it also has been largely criticized [49]. We also used *precision*, *recall*, and ϕ, to have a more comprehensive picture about the performance of the tools we used.

5   Related Work

Tools that use static analysis to identify likely defective code have been introduced more than twenty years ago. Several research efforts have been devoted to investigating their real effectiveness.

Rahman et al. [35] compared the defect prediction capabilities of static analysis tools (namely FindBugs, PMD, and Jlint) and statistical defect prediction based on historical data.

Vetrò et al. [47] evaluated the accuracy of FindBugs. The code base used for the evaluation consisted of Java projects developed by students during a programming course. The code is equipped with acceptance tests written by teachers of the course to check all functionalities. To determine true positives, they used temporal and spatial coincidence: an issue was considered related to a bug when it disappeared at the same time as a bug got fixed. Later, Vetrò et al. repeated the analysis, with a larger code set and performing inspections concerning four types of issues found by FindBugs, namely the types of findings considered more reliable [46].

Zazworka et al. studied the relationship between technical debt items reported by developers and the indications provided by FindBugs [52]. They found that FindBugs did well in pointing to source code files with defect debt. However, finer granularity evaluations do not seem to have been addressed.

Danphitsanuphan and Suwantada studied the correlation between code smells and some structural problems reported by FindBugs [11]. However, they did not check whether the structural problems correspond to actual defects.

Zazworka et al. [51] also applied four different technical debt identification techniques (including code smells and automatic static analysis) to 13 versions of an open-source software project. Noticeably, the outputs of the four approaches pointed to different problems in the source code. The research method used by Zazworka et al. [51] is quite different from ours. They looked for correlations between issues reported by tools and actions on code connected with repaying the interests of technical debt. By considering a sufficiently long streak of versions, they obtained a good representation of the underlying relationships between reported issues and the technical debt. Our approach is inherently different. We consider a single version of many software products and manually inspect the code that SpotBugs flags as possibly defective. In this way, we verify whether issues reported by the static analysis tool are actual defects or not.

Thung et al. performed an empirical study to evaluate to what extent field defects could be detected by FindBugs and similar tools [41]. To this end, Find-Bugs was applied to three open-source programs (Lucene, Rhino and AspectJ). The study by Thung et al. takes into consideration only known bugs. On the contrary, we relied on manual inspection to identify actual bugs.

In 2007, Ayewah et al. evaluated the issues found by FindBugs in production software developed by Sun and Google [7]. They classified the found issues into false positives, trivial bugs, and serious bugs. A substantial fraction of the issues turned out to concern real but trivial problems. Accordingly, they stated that "Trying to devise static analysis techniques that suppress or deprioritize true defects with minimal impact, and high-light defects with significant impact, is an important and interesting research question." 13 years later, we wish to check if SpotBugs (the heir of FindBugs) has improved in detecting "important" issues.

Vestola applied FindBugs to Valuatum's system and found that 18.5% of the issues were real bugs that deserved corrections, 77.6% were mostly harmless bugs, and 3.8% were false positives [45].

Kim and Ernst evaluated the relationship between issues reported by three static analysis tools (including FindBugs) and the history of changes in three open source products [21]. They consider warnings that remain in the programs or are removed during non-fix changes as likely false positive warnings. Although it is probably so, it is hardly so for all such warnings, hence the number of false positives is likely overestimated.

Code smell were defined by Fowler et al. in 1999 [16], based on previous work [8,36]. A few years later, Marinescu proposed to identify smells on the basis of static code measures [27]: since then, several tools implementing automatic code smell detection—both based on Marinescu's definitions and on other definitions—have been developed, such as Decor, CodeVizard, JDeodorant, etc. [9,28,29,43,44,50].

Many researchers addressed the problem of verifying to what extent code smells are associated with code problems that can affect external code qualities (mainly maintainability and correctness). Lately, a few Systematic Literature Reviews (SLR) were published [20,32,33,37], summarizing the evidence collected about code smell harmfulness. The mentioned SLRs depict a situation characterized by several studies, which produced evidence that does not seem conclusive.

6   Conclusions

In this paper, we have described an empirical study that we carried out to assess the usefulness of static analysis and code smell detection in the identification of bugs. Our study uses two popular tools, SpotBugs and JDeodorant, which are applied to a limited set of OSS projects. The study shows that these tools can help software practitioners detect and remove defects in an effective way, to limit the amount of resources that would otherwise be spent in more cost-intensive activities, such as software inspections.

SpotBugs appears to detect defects with good *precision*, hence manual inspection of the code flagged defective by SpotBugs becomes cost-effective. When JDeodorant is used in conjunction with SpotBugs, detection *precision* increases, thus making manual code inspections even more effective. However, *recall* decreases, thus decreasing the number of bugs that are actually identified.

References

1. FindBugs website (2020). http://findbugs.sourceforge.net/
2. JDeodorant website (2020). https://github.com/tsantalis/JDeodorant
3. SpotBugs documentation website (2020). https://spotbugs.readthedocs.io/en/latest/
4. SpotBugs website (2020). https://spotbugs.github.io/
5. Ackerman, A.F., Buchwald, L.S., Lewski, F.H.: Software inspections: an effective verification process. IEEE Softw. **6**(3), 31–36 (1989)
6. Aurum, A., Petersson, H., Wohlin, C.: State-of-the-art: software inspections after 25 years. Softw. Test. Verification Reliab. **12**(3), 133–154 (2002)
7. Ayewah, N., Pugh, W., Morgenthaler, J.D., Penix, J., Zhou, Y.: Evaluating static analysis defect warnings on production software (2007)
8. Brown, W.H., Malveau, R.C., McCormick, H.W.S., Mowbray, T.J.: AntiPatterns: Refactoring Software, Architectures, and Projects in Crisis, 1st edn. Wiley, New York (1998)
9. Codoban, M., Marinescu, C., Marinescu, R.: iProblems-an integrated instrument for reporting design flaws, vulnerabilities and defects. In: 2011 18th Working Conference on Reverse Engineering, pp. 437–438. IEEE (2011)
10. Cohen, J.: Statistical Power Analysis for the Behavioral Sciences. Lawrence Earlbaum Associates Routledge, New York (1988)

11. Danphitsanuphan, P., Suwantada, T.: Code smell detecting tool and code smell-structure bug relationship. In: 2012 Spring Congress on Engineering and Technology, pp. 1–5. IEEE (2012)
12. Fagan, M.E.: Design and code inspections to reduce errors in program development. IBM Syst. J. **38**, 258–287 (1976)
13. Fagan, M.E.: Advances in software inspections. In: Broy, M., Denert, E. (eds.) Pioneers and Their Contributions to Software Engineering, pp. 335–360. Springer, Heidelberg (2001). https://doi.org/10.1007/978-3-642-48354-7_14
14. Fokaefs, M., Tsantalis, N., Chatzigeorgiou, A.: JDeodorant: identification and removal of feature envy bad smells. In: 2007 IEEE International Conference on Software Maintenance, pp. 519–520 (2007)
15. Fokaefs, M., Tsantalis, N., Chatzigeorgiou, A.: JDeodorant: identification and removal of feature envy bad smells. In: 2007 IEEE International Conference on Software Maintenance, pp. 519–520. IEEE (2007)
16. Fowler, M., Beck, K., Brant, J., Opdyke, W., Roberts, D.: Refactoring: Improving the Design of Existing Code. Addison-Wesley Professional, Boston (1999)
17. Hall, T., Zhang, M., Bowes, D., Sun, Y.: Some code smells have a significant but small effect on faults. ACM Trans. Softw. Eng. Methodol. (TOSEM) **23**(4), 1–39 (2014)
18. Hernández-Orallo, J., Flach, P., Ferri, C.: A unified view of performance metrics: translating threshold choice into expected classification loss. J. Mach. Learn. Res. **13**, 2813–2869 (2012)
19. Hovemeyer, D., Pugh, W.: Finding bugs is easy. ACM SIGPLAN Not. **39**(12), 92–106 (2004)
20. Kaur, A.: A systematic literature review on empirical analysis of the relationship between code smells and software quality attributes. Arch. Comput. Methods Eng. **27**, 1267–1296 (2019)
21. Kim, S., Ernst, M.D.: Which warnings should I fix first? In: 6th Joint Meeting of the European Software Engineering Conference and the ACM SIGSOFT Symposium on the Foundations of Software Engineering, pp. 45–54 (2007)
22. Lavazza, L.: Software quality evaluation via static analysis and static measurement: an industrial experience. In: The Fifteenth International Conference on Software Engineering Advances - ICSEA 2020, pp. 55–60 (2020)
23. Lavazza, L., Morasca, S., Tosi, D.: An empirical study on the factors affecting software development productivity. e-Informatica Softw. Eng. J. **12**(1), 27–49 (2018). https://doi.org/10.5277/e-Inf180102
24. Lavazza, L., Tosi, D., Morasca, S.: An empirical study on the persistence of Spot-Bugs issues in open-source software evolution. In: Shepperd, M., Brito e Abreu, F., Rodrigues da Silva, A., Pérez-Castillo, R. (eds.) QUATIC 2020. CCIS, vol. 1266, pp. 144–151. Springer, Cham (2020). https://doi.org/10.1007/978-3-030-58793-2_12
25. Lenarduzzi, V., Taibi, D., Tosi, D., Lavazza, L., Morasca, S.: Open source software evaluation, selection, and adoption: a systematic literature review. In: 46th Euromicro Conference on Software Engineering and Advanced Applications (SEAA), pp. 437–444 (2020)
26. Lenarduzzi, V., Tosi, D., Lavazza, L., Morasca, S.: Why do developers adopt open source software? past, present and future. In: In: Bordeleau F., Sillitti A., Meirelles P., Lenarduzzi V. (eds.) Open Source Systems. OSS 2019. IFIP International Conference on Open Source Systems, pp. 104–115. Springer, Cham (2019). https://doi.org/10.1007/978-3-030-20883-7_10

27. Marinescu, R.: Detection strategies: metrics-based rules for detecting design flaws. In: 20th IEEE International Conference on Software Maintenance, pp. 350–359. IEEE (2004)
28. Moha, N., Gueheneuc, Y.G., Duchien, L., Le Meur, A.F.: DECOR: a method for the specification and detection of code and design smells. IEEE Trans. Softw. Eng. **36**(1), 20–36 (2009)
29. Murphy-Hill, E., Black, A.P.: An interactive ambient visualization for code smells. In: 5th International Symposium on Software Visualization, pp. 5–14 (2010)
30. Olbrich, S.M., Cruzes, D.S., Sjøberg, D.I.: Are all code smells harmful? a study of god classes and brain classes in the evolution of three open source systems. In: 2010 IEEE International Conference on Software Maintenance, pp. 1–10. IEEE (2010)
31. Palomba, F., Bavota, G., Di Penta, M., Fasano, F., Oliveto, R., De Lucia, A.: On the diffuseness and the impact on maintainability of code smells: a large scale empirical investigation. Empirical Softw. Eng. **23**(3), 1188–1221 (2018)
32. de Paulo Sobrinho, E.V., De Lucia, A., de Almeida Maia, M.: A systematic literature review on bad smells—5 w's: which, when, what, who, where. IEEE Trans. Softw. Eng. **47**(1), 17–66 (2021)
33. Piotrowski, P., Madeyski, L.: Software defect prediction using bad code smells: a systematic literature review. In: Poniszewska-Marańda, A., Kryvinska, N., Jarząbek, S., Madeyski, L. (eds.) Data-Centric Business and Applications. LNDECT, vol. 40, pp. 77–99. Springer, Cham (2020). https://doi.org/10.1007/978-3-030-34706-2_5
34. Powers, D.M.: Evaluation: from precision, recall and F-measure to ROC, informedness, markedness and correlation (2011)
35. Rahman, F., Khatri, S., Barr, E.T., Devanbu, P.: Comparing static bug finders and statistical prediction. In: 36th International Conference on Software Engineering, pp. 424–434 (2014)
36. Riel, A.J.: Object-Oriented Design Heuristics, vol. 335. Addison-Wesley, Reading (1996)
37. Santos, J.A.M., Rocha-Junior, J.B., Prates, L.C.L., do Nascimento, R.S., Freitas, M.F., de Mendonça, M.G.: A systematic review on the code smell effect. J. Syst. Softw. **144**, 450–477 (2018)
38. Schumacher, J., Zazworka, N., Shull, F., Seaman, C., Shaw, M.: Building empirical support for automated code smell detection. In: ACM-IEEE International Symposium on Empirical Software Engineering and Measurement, pp. 1–10 (2010)
39. Shen, H., Fang, J., Zhao, J.: EFindbugs: effective error ranking for findbugs. In: 2011 Fourth IEEE International Conference on Software Testing, Verification and Validation, pp. 299–308. IEEE (2011)
40. Sjøberg, D.I., Yamashita, A., Anda, B.C., Mockus, A., Dybå, T.: Quantifying the effect of code smells on maintenance effort. IEEE Trans. Softw. Eng. **39**(8), 1144–1156 (2012)
41. Thung, F., Lo, D., Jiang, L., Rahman, F., Devanbu, P.T., et al.: To what extent could we detect field defects? An extended empirical study of false negatives in static bug-finding tools. Autom. Softw. Eng. **22**(4), 561–602 (2015)
42. Tsantalis, N., Chaikalis, T., Chatzigeorgiou, A.: JDeodorant: identification and removal of type-checking bad smells. In: 2008 12th European Conference on Software Maintenance and Reengineering, pp. 329–331. IEEE (2008)
43. Tsantalis, N., Chatzigeorgiou, A.: Identification of extract method refactoring opportunities for the decomposition of methods. J. Syst. Softw. **84**(10), 1757–1782 (2011)

44. Van Emden, E., Moonen, L.: Java quality assurance by detecting code smells. In: Ninth Working Conference on Reverse Engineering, pp. 97–106. IEEE (2002)
45. Vestola, M., et al.: Evaluating and enhancing findbugs to detect bugs from mature software; case study in valuatum (2012)
46. Vetrò, A., Morisio, M., Torchiano, M.: An empirical validation of findbugs issues related to defects. In: 15th Annual Conference on Evaluation and Assessment in Software Engineering (EASE 2011), pp. 144–153. IET (2011)
47. Vetrò, A., Torchiano, M., Morisio, M.: Assessing the precision of FindBugs by mining java projects developed at a university. In: 2010 7th IEEE Working Conference on Mining Software Repositories (MSR 2010), pp. 110–113. IEEE (2010)
48. Yamashita, A.: Assessing the capability of code smells to explain maintenance problems: an empirical study combining quantitative and qualitative data. Empirical Softw. Eng. 19(4), 1111–1143 (2014)
49. Yao, J., Shepperd, M.J.: Assessing software defection prediction performance: why using the Matthews correlation coefficient matters. In: Evaluation and Assessment in Software Engineering, EASE 2020, Trondheim, Norway, 15–17 April 2020, pp. 120–129. ACM (2020)
50. Zazworka, N., Ackermann, C.: CodeVizard: a tool to aid the analysis of software evolution. In: Proceedings of the 2010 ACM-IEEE International Symposium on Empirical Software Engineering and Measurement, pp. 1–1 (2010)
51. Zazworka, N., Izurieta, C., Wong, S., Cai, Y., Seaman, C., Shull, F., et al.: Comparing four approaches for technical debt identification. Softw. Q. J. 22(3), 403–426 (2014)
52. Zazworka, N., Spínola, R.O., Vetrò, A., Shull, F., Seaman, C.: A case study on effectively identifying technical debt. In: Proceedings of the 17th International Conference on Evaluation and Assessment in Software Engineering, pp. 42–47 (2013)

Enabling OSS Usage Through Procurement Projects: How Can Lock-in Effects Be Avoided?

Björn Lundell[1]([⊠]), Jonas Gamalielsson[1], Simon Butler[1], Christoffer Brax[2],
Tomas Persson[3], Anders Mattsson[4], Tomas Gustavsson[5], Jonas Feist[6],
and Jonas Öberg[7]

[1] University of Skövde, Skövde, Sweden
{bjorn.lundell,jonas.gamalielsson,simon.butler}@his.se
[2] Combitech AB, Skövde, Sweden
christoffer.brax@combitech.com
[3] Digitalist Sweden AB, Stockholm, Sweden
tomas.persson@digitalistgroup.com
[4] Husqvarna AB, Huskvarna, Sweden
anders.mattsson@husqvarnagroup.com
[5] PrimeKey Solutions AB, Solna, Sweden
tomas.gustavsson@primekey.com
[6] RedBridge AB, Stockholm, Sweden
jfeist@redbridge.se
[7] Scania CV AB, Södertälje, Sweden
jonas.oberg@scania.com

Abstract. Formulation of mandatory requirements in procurement projects has significant influence on opportunities for development and deployment of Open Source Software (OSS). The paper contributes insights on a widespread practice amongst public procurement projects which causes problematic lock-in effects and thereby inhibits opportunities for use of OSS solutions. Through a systematic investigation of 30 randomly selected procurement projects in the software domain the paper highlights illustrative examples of mandatory requirements which cause lock-in and presents five recommendations for how requirements instead should be formulated in order to avoid causing lock-in. Findings show significant lock-in caused by current procurement practices with a stark preference for proprietary software and SaaS solutions amongst procuring organisations.

Keywords: Open source software projects · Procurement projects ·
IT-standards · Open standards · Lock-in effects

1 Introduction

Investigations of a large number of IT procurement projects have identified widespread practices amongst public sector organisations that cause different lock-in effects which

© IFIP International Federation for Information Processing 2021
Published by Springer Nature Switzerland AG 2021
D. Taibi et al. (Eds.): OSS 2021, IFIP AICT 624, pp. 16–27, 2021.
https://doi.org/10.1007/978-3-030-75251-4_2

in turn inhibit Open Source Software (OSS) usage [29]. Further, it is far from uncommon that procurement projects express mandatory requirements which refer to specific IT standards that prevent implementation in OSS projects [17, 25, 29]. In turn, if an organisation expresses a requirement for an IT standard which inhibits implementation and use of OSS such a practice causes lock-in that inhibits competition. As stated by Katz [23]: "Lock-in has been recognized as distorting the market process, creating unfair monopolies for the participants."

With increased adoption and use of proprietary licenced Software as a Service (SaaS) solutions, researchers and policy makers have recognised lock-in effects as a significant concern [19, 20, 33]. For example, the GAIA-X initiative states that lock-in effects "can be of a technical-functional kind (dependence on the specific features of certain providers); they can arise from contractual agreements (e.g. license models and penalty costs), but also result from a high, customer-specific degree of personalisation, from familiarisation effects, or from the sheer data volume that is to be migrated." [19].

Amongst policy recommendations for an organisation that seeks to avoid lock-in related to usage of a SaaS solution, the importance of conduct of a careful review of all contract terms for the solution has been stressed with a recommendation to avoid accepting terms which allow the provider of the solution to unilaterally change contract terms and ensuring availability of an effective exit strategy [13]. Further, concerning procurement of software applications it has been recommended that "compatibility with proprietary technologies should be explicitly excluded from public procurement criteria and replaced by interoperability with products from multiple vendors." [21].

The *overarching goal* of the study is to illuminate how current practice in procurement projects impacts on opportunities for development and deployment of OSS that implement IT standards. The study investigates the following research questions:

RQ1: How do public sector organisations express mandatory requirements on development and deployment of software which impact on opportunities for use of OSS?

RQ2: How are requirements on IT-standards expressed in public procurement projects and how should they be modified in order to avoid lock-in effects and allow for strategic use of OSS?

2   On Lock-in Effects in the Software Domain

Related to different technologies several studies have addressed different types of lock-in effects [1, 5, 16]. For example, previous research shows that 'historical events' can lead to lock-in [1]. One historical example being touch typing that 'gave rise to three features of the evolving production system which were crucially important in causing QWERTY to become "locked in" as the dominant keyboard arrangement. These features were technical interrelatedness, economies of scale, and quasi-irreversibility of investment.' [5].

OSS projects and IT standards, and in particular the role of OSS for implementing standards, have been recognised as important enablers for addressing lock-in effects. For example, outcomes from an EU study claim that contributing "to OSS is perceived as a strategy to prevent proprietary software solutions, which might create a vendor lock-in and consequently closes markets instead of opening them" [2]. Further, the study stresses that when an organisation contributes its own code of high quality to OSS such work practices are perceived as a contribution to a common good and that such work practices also promote the own organisation's autonomy and control of its own software development [2].

Policy makers in different countries have presented a number of policy recommendations related to use of IT standards [6–10, 12, 31, 32, 34–36]. Further, the EU has presented a catalogue of ICT standards which are recommended for use in 20 different European countries [9, 12]. Several of the standards included in these recommendations allow for implementation in OSS as they fulfil the definition of an open standard which is presented by the European Interoperability Framework version 1.0 [6]. For example, all standards included in the recommendation presented in Sweden are open IT standards [32], whereas research shows that some standards recommended for use in some other countries (e.g. the JPEG 2000 standard and several MPEG-standards) are closed standards which inhibit implementation in OSS [27]. Further, all framework contracts for public procurement projects established by the Swedish National Procurement Services (a governmental agency) at Kammarkollegiet [32] require that any reference to a standard in a mandatory requirement in a procurement project must conform to the EU definition of an open standard [6]. Requirements for open standards with the same [31] or similar [34–36] definition have been included in national policy established in other countries in order to allow for use of OSS and promote software interoperability.

3   Research Approach

The study addresses how current practice in procurement projects impacts on opportunities for development and deployment of OSS that implement IT standards through investigation of 30 randomly selected procurement projects undertaken by Swedish municipalities in 2019. The investigation considered procurement projects that have been publicly announced in Tenders Electronic Daily (an EU public procurement service) if it included at least one of the two Common Procurement Vocabulary (CPV) codes (in divisions 48 and 72) for 'software package and information systems' and 'IT services: consulting, software development, Internet and support'.

Central government has limited influence on Swedish municipalities' public procurement projects as municipalities have significant autonomy with respect to conduct of public procurement. The vast majority (94%) of the 290 Swedish municipalities have fewer than 100,000 citizens and the median sized municipality has approximately 16,000 citizens. Hence, many public procurement projects are undertaken by rather small, independent municipalities, even though many challenges related to digitalisation and IT are very similar amongst municipalities.

For each investigated procurement project, we reviewed tender documents and analysed each mandatory requirement with a view to identify any explicit (or implicit) reference to IT standards which may impact on opportunities for a potential supplier to provide a bid which includes an OSS solution. The coding of documentation from each procurement project was conducted in a manner which follows Glaser's ideas on open coding [24]. We specifically considered the formulation of each mandatory requirement which may cause any (intentional or unintentional) lock-in and thereby also restrict competition as an unintended consequence for the procuring organisation by inhibiting some potential suppliers from submitting bids.

Amongst the 30 investigated public procurement projects we found that documentation from the vast majority of the selected procurement projects refer to a range of different technologies and explicitly refer to specific proprietary software. For example, amongst procurement projects municipalities request solutions, such as: a student administration system and learning platform for public schools; a scheduling system for public schools; an IT-solution for digital tests; a document and case management system with an e-archive solution; a system for health and social care; a video conference system with support for e-voting; a system for distribution of invoices; a debt collection system; a cloud based web platform for a website; a Customer support system; a HR and salary system; consultants for software development related to Geographical Information Systems (GIS); and a GIS-system.

For a selected set of the problematic mandatory requirements, as identified from the outcome of our analysis of each mandatory requirement, we present five recommendations for improved (alternative) formulations of the mandatory requirements which we claim will significantly improve the situation and (most likely) avoid problematic lock-in effects. The evolved recommendations are grounded in a comprehensive analysis of current practice concerning expression of mandatory requirements in procurement projects and supplemented by a literature analysis which informed the formulation of each recommendation. The formulation of the recommendation also benefited from that several authors of this study have extensive prior experiences and insights from analysis of, and direct involvement in procurement projects in different roles, including previous research which has analysed and contributed to procurement projects.

4 Results

This section presents results concerning how public sector organisations express mandatory requirements on development and deployment of software which impact on opportunities for use of OSS (Subsect. 4.1). Thereafter, the section presents results concerning how mandatory requirements expressed in public procurement projects cause lock-in effects which impact on opportunities for strategic use of OSS (Subsect. 4.2). Specifically, illustrative examples of how mandatory requirements that cause lock-in effects are expressed in procurement projects are presented, together with suggested modified alternative formulations for expressing each requirement in order to avoid lock-in and allow for strategic use of OSS.

4.1 Development and Deployment of Software Impacting on Opportunities for OSS Usage

Software development projects can provide software under a number of different conditions, including terms which fulfil the Open Source Definition (OSD) that have been recognised as OSS licences by the Open Source Initiative (OSI). Further, software provided under other terms is often referred to as proprietary software (and sometimes closed source software). Software can be deployed in a number of different ways, for example through internal deployment which may involve installation and use of a software application on a local computer (on premise). Further, a software application which is deployed and installed on a server that is controlled by some external organisation may provide the application as a public SaaS solution. In this latter scenario the procuring organisation typically uses the externally deployed public SaaS solution via a web browser.

A conceptualisation of four principal ways for *development of software* (open *or* closed) and *deployment of software* (internal *or* external) is presented in Fig. 1. From the perspective of the procuring organisation, development of software which is provided as OSS may be internally deployed (lower left quadrant of Fig. 1) or be externally deployed (lower right quadrant of Fig. 1). Similarly, development of software which is provided as proprietary software may be internally deployed (upper left quadrant of Fig. 1) or be externally deployed (upper right quadrant of Fig. 1). To further clarify the conceptualisation, illustrative examples of software applications of each type are presented in Fig. 1. From the perspective of a procuring organisation it should be noted that several OSS projects develop and provide OSS (e.g. Nextcloud) which can be deployed both internally and externally. For example, the SaaS solution Nextcloud can be provided to the procuring organisation through internal deployment (e.g. Nextcloud can be internally used by the procuring organisation through provision by the organisation's own IT department). Further, Nextcloud can also be provided to the procuring organisation through deployment by an external organisation as a public SaaS solution (e.g. Nextcloud can be provided by a global company).

| | | Deployment of software ... | |
		Internal	External
Development of software ...	**Closed**	e.g. **Microsoft Office 2019**	e.g. **Microsoft 365**
	Open	e.g. **LibreOffice, Nextcloud**	e.g. **Nextcloud**

Fig. 1. Conceptualising four principal ways for development and deployment of software

Concerning *development of software* applications, procurement projects express stark preference for proprietary software solutions. The vast majority (90%) of the investigated projects express one or several mandatory requirements which discriminate against provision of OSS solutions. We find a widespread practice of explicitly (or implicitly) referring to specific vendors, specific proprietary software applications which are provided and controlled by specific companies. Further, we also find a widespread practice amongst procurement projects to include mandatory requirements which request compatibility (instead of interoperability) with specific technologies. For example, procurement projects include compatibility requirements with reference to one (or several) of the following: AD (Active Directory), EPIserver DXC (a cloud based CMS solution), iPad, Microsoft Office 365, Oracle DB, and Stratsys (a cloud based strategic planning solution). In addition, several projects express mandatory requirements which request integration with proprietary software applications and technology. For example, amongst analysed projects we find mandatory requirements for integration with one (or several) of the following: iipax (a proprietary e-archiving solution), Microsoft BizTalk 2016, Phoniro's locking solution (for Senior Care), Sharepoint, Stratsys, and TEIS (an integration platform server). Overall, we find that such procurement practices inhibit opportunities for potential suppliers to offer OSS solutions.

The remaining (10%) procurement projects lack explicitly expressed mandatory requirements related to software. One of these remaining procurement projects (which requested an administrative system for primary schools, expressed only (high-level) functionality requirements. In another procurement projects (requesting a system for invoice distribution), the procurement project made reference to several proprietary software applications from which data should be processed by the procured application (and based on the limited information provided it is unclear if it is possible for a potential supplier to offer a bid for an OSS solution). Further, in yet another case, the procuring organisation expressed requirements for IT consultants which are focused on one specific global provider.

Concerning *deployment of software* applications, we find that almost half (47%) of the analysed procurement projects do not express any requirements for how a procured application shall be deployed. Further, amongst the procurement projects which express requirements for how a procured software application shall be deployed we find a clear preference for deployment of the procured application in an external organisation as a cloud or SaaS solution.

Specifically, amongst the analysed procurement projects we find that more than one out of three (37%) projects include a mandatory requirement which expresses that the software application must be deployed as a cloud or a SaaS solution in an external organisation (e.g. expressed as that the system 'shall be provided as a cloud solution' or as 'the application shall be of the type SaaS solution' with the requirement that the operation shall be included), whereas only one out of ten (10%) require that the software application must be internally deployed in the procuring organisation as an on premise solution (e.g. expressed as the 'system shall be installed locally'). Hence, amongst (almost half of) the procurement projects which actually express a requirement for how the procured software application shall be deployed we find a clear preference for deployment of the procured application as a cloud or SaaS solution at an external organisation.

In addition, some (7%) of the analysed procurement projects require that a procured software application must be both internally and externally deployed. This implies that for those projects the procured application will be both internally provided in the procuring organisation and also as a cloud or a SaaS solution that is provided by an external organisation.

Almost all procurement projects which procure a SaaS solution do not consider licensing and legal aspects (including the GDPR) when expressing mandatory requirements concerning processing and maintenance of the procuring organisation's data. This is despite procuring a SaaS solution which, when used, will process personal data. Only one procurement project requires that maintenance and processing of personal data must take place in the EU/EES by a legal entity which is represented in the EU/EES. However, none of the procurement projects express any mandatory requirements related to applicable laws for contracting parties (e.g. if a procuring organisation requires that all parties involved with the data processing are bound by Swedish law) and under which law (e.g. only Swedish and EU law) data processing are allowed to take place when a procured SaaS solution is used (e.g. if processing of personal data in certain third countries are disallowed).

4.2   Requirements on IT Standards Impacting on Lock-in Effects

Some procurement projects make reference to open standards and open formats when expressing mandatory requirements. For example, we find one procurement project which requires that all integration between IT systems use open standards and another project expressing a mandatory requirement for 'open and standardised formats' related to provision of personal data in connection with a future exit from a procured SaaS solution. Further, several procurement projects refer to specific IT standards when expressing mandatory requirements. Several projects refer to specific IT standards (e.g. ODF, PNG, PDF/A-1, XML, HTML5, and CSV) which comply with the definition of open standard [6, 32]. However, there are several projects which refer (in some cases in a somewhat unclear way) to specific IT standards and file formats (e.g. MPEG, MPEG4, DWG, PDF/A-2, and Microsoft formats) that do not constitute open standards [6].

Amongst analysed procurement projects which include explicitly expressed mandatory requirements related to software we find many implicit and indirect references (in many cases referenced via specific implementations in software) to a range of different IT standards. Amongst implicit references to specific IT standards we find many projects which include mandatory requirements expressed by reference to specific file format standards through its filename extension, such as: 'docx', 'dwg', 'jpeg', 'png', and 'mpeg4'. Further, amongst indirect references to specific IT standards expressed via implementation of the standards in specifically referenced software applications (including several SaaS solutions) we find several unclear mandatory requirements.

Several procurement projects include mandatory requirements which refer to specific proprietary technologies that by some procuring organisations are perceived as 'standards' even though these are not recognised by any standards setting organisation. In many cases such proprietary technologies are controlled by a specific company, such as for example 'AD' (Active Directory, a directory service developed for Microsoft Windows). On the other hand, we also find some procurement projects which refer to OSS projects (e.g. Apache Tomcat and LibreOffice) and projects which express a mandatory requirement for the availability of OSS that can interpret files that need to be maintained and processed by a procuring organisation.

Many procurement projects express mandatory requirements with reference to specific implementations in software. For example, one project expressed a mandatory requirement which required 'PDF from Raindance' (based on the information provided by this procurement project it is unclear how, and which version of the PDF file format is used by this specific SaaS solution for creation of PDF files). Similarly, another project expressed that support for exporting data from the procured application 'to the Google docs format' in a mandatory requirement (without providing any details concerning how 'the' technical specification for the format used internally by the SaaS solution is actually specified and implemented). Further, several procurement projects express (in many cases rather vaguely formulated) mandatory requirements that request integration and compatibility with the file formats used by 'iWork', 'Office 365', and 'MS Office'.

Overall, from analysis of all mandatory requirements expressed in the investigated procurement projects, we observe stark confusion related to the difference between software application on the one hand, and IT standards (and file formats) on the other. Some procurement projects include mandatory requirements which make explicit references to formal standards. For example, one project referred to a withdrawn standard (ISO/IEC 10646:2003) when expressing a mandatory requirement. In this case, we note that several successive editions of the standard (i.e. ISO/IEC 10646:2011, ISO/IEC 10646:2012 and ISO/IEC 10646:2014) have also been withdrawn and that the fifth edition of this standard (ISO/IEC 10646:2017) is under review.

Based on our analysis of the investigated procurement projects we present five actionable recommendations for preventing lock-in effects for any procuring organisation that expresses mandatory requirements in procurement projects.

First, a procuring organisation needs to express requirements for interoperability with open IT standards (instead of compatibility with a specific proprietary technology which is controlled by a single provider). We find that if an organisation expresses a requirement for compatibility with a specific proprietary software application such practice contributes to lock-in. There is strong support for this recommendation in EU law and previous studies [17, 21, 25, 29, 33].

Second, a procuring organisation needs to express requirements for open IT standards (instead of closed IT standards) in order to avoid lock-in. There is strong support for this recommendation in previous research [2, 11, 19, 21, 26, 27] and reports from policy makers at different levels [7, 8, 10, 34–36]. Further, if an organisation expresses a requirement for a closed IT standard, it may (for both legal and technical reasons) be impossible to implement this standard in OSS [27].

Third, a procuring organisation should express requirements for an IT standard only if it has been implemented by one or several OSS projects. If sustainable OSS projects faithfully implement a specific IT standard in OSS this minimise the risk for being unable to interpret digital assets previously created in the specific IT standard. We find that if there is no publicly available OSS implementation for a specific IT standard this imposes significant risks for lock-in, and it may be a sign that there are technical and legal issues with the standard itself. There are many technical, legal and business related challenges which impact on the possibility to develop software applications which conform to technical specifications of specific IT standards [2, 4, 11, 19, 21, 26, 27, 30].

Fourth, a procuring organisation needs to avoid expressing requirements for specific proprietary software applications that cause problematic lock-in for the procuring organisations. There is strong support for this recommendation in Swedish and EU law [25]. We find that if an organisation expresses a requirement for a proprietary licenced software application this imposes risks for the procuring organisation (e.g. risks related to long-term maintenance and reuse of digital assets created through use of the procured software application) which need to be carefully considered in each case.

Fifth, a procuring organisation needs to develop an effective exit strategy which allows for abandoning the procured software application (and in particular if the application is deployed as a SaaS solution provided by an external organisation) on short notice with preserved data and digital assets which can be reused in open file formats. There is strong support for this recommendation in policy recommendations [13] and previous research [28]. For example, one of the policy recommendations included in a checklist presented by eSam states: "Is there a strategy that allows or abandoning the cloud service in the future (an exit plan)?" [13]. Further, lock-in and availability of an effective exit strategy is considered as one of the "top concerns with the cloud" [22]. We find that if an organisation expresses a requirement without considering the possibility to undertake an effective exit from day one, this imposes risks for the procuring organisation which need to be carefully considered in each case.

5 Discussion and Conclusions

Based on analysis of the mandatory requirements expressed in the investigated procurement projects, we find widespread lack of clarity and significant scope for improvement related to expressing competition neutral, relevant and unambiguous mandatory requirements amongst procuring organisations. For example, several procurement projects have confused specific software applications with specific IT standards when expressing mandatory requirements. Further, many projects have expressed mandatory requirements without having understood the fundamental difference between a technical specification of a specific IT standard which is implemented in a specific software application (that is provided by a software project), and the same specification (of the same IT standard) as documented in a standard document (that is provided by a standard setting organisation, e.g. ISO). When comparing to previous studies undertaken in the Swedish context which have identified problematic procurement practices that cause lock-in [25, 29] we find that previously identified problematic practices remain and even have become even more problematic. We conjecture that this, at least partly, may be explained by an increased proportion of problematic mandatory requirements expressed in relation to procurement of SaaS solutions.

Related to the evolved recommendations for preventing lock-in when undertaking procurement projects, we find that providers of SaaS solutions may cause a range of lock-in challenges for a customer which consequently may need to recover its externally maintained data on short notice, perhaps due to that the provider decides to change the contract terms or in case of serious problems for the provider which leads to a discontinued solution. For example, we note that a cloud solution provider gave its customers "two weeks to get their data back" [3].

For these reasons it may be unsurprising that a number of policy recommendations which seek to address these, and related, challenges have been presented over the years. For example, eSam (a collaboration between 29 central government agencies and the Swedish Association of Local Authorities and Regions, which represents all 290 Swedish municipalities [15]) has presented recommendations related to use of cloud and SaaS solutions, including a legal analysis [14] in addition to its checklist which contains recommendations to an organisation related to procurement of cloud solutions [13].

Further, an analysis undertaken by Swedish legal experts argues that, under normal conditions, it is unlawful for a Swedish public sector organisation to enter into a contract with a supplier, for example for procurement and use of a SaaS solution, in cases where any foreign law may impact the public sector organisation's ability to ensure official tasks are performed according to Swedish law [18]. Further, this may, inter alia, concern data processing and official duties to ensure information is preserved in data formats suitable for archival purposes, or that rules governing public access to information and secrecy are in fact observed so that information cannot improperly be given to a third party such as a foreign government. The authors argue that it would in these cases be in contravention of the obligation in the Swedish legal order, for authorities to give rules in a foreign jurisdiction precedence over the Swedish legal order [18]. Based on these arguments, we find that this should be the case regardless of whether the authority enters into a contract directly with an international cloud service provider, or whether the authority enters into a contract with a Swedish SaaS provider which in turn relies on an international IaaS provider, as the same fundamental issue can persist in either case.

In conclusion, based on analysis of all mandatory requirements in the investigated procurement projects we find a widespread practice amongst procuring organisations to include explicit references to specific proprietary technologies and IT standards which do not comply with the EU definition of an open standard that is also used by the National Procurement Services in Sweden. Consequently, to avoid lock-in effects and promote software interoperability we find that procuring organisations need to promote use of open IT standards which can be (and already are) implemented in OSS by sustainable OSS projects. For reasons of sustainable digitalisation, we find improved public procurement practices to be critical for avoiding an unintentional discrimination against development and deployment of effective OSS solutions.

Acknowledgements. This research has been financially supported by the Swedish Knowledge Foundation (KK-stiftelsen) and participating partner organisations in the SUDO project. The authors are grateful for the stimulating collaboration and support from colleagues and partner organisations.

References

1. Arthur, B.: Competing technologies, increasing returns, and lock-in by historical events. Econ. J. **99**(394), 116–131 (1989)
2. Blind, K., Böhm, M.: The relationship between open source software and standard setting. In: Thumm, N. (ed.) EUR 29867 EN, JRC (Joint Research Centre) Science for Policy Report, Publications Office of the European Union, Luxembourg, ISBN 978-92-76-11593-9 (2019)
3. Butler, B.: Gartner analyst's advice to customers of shuttering Nirvanix: PANIC!, Cloud Chronicles Netw. World (2013)
4. Butler, S., et al.: Maintaining interoperability in open source software: a case study of the Apache PDFBox project. J. Syst. Softw. **159**, 110452 (2020)
5. David, P.A.: Clio and the economics of QWERTY. Am. Econ. Rev. **75**(2), 332–337 (1985)
6. EC: European Interoperability Framework for Pan-European eGovernment Services, Version 1.0. European Commission, ISBN 92-894-8389-X (2004)

7. EC: Against lock-in: building open ICT systems by making better use of standards in public procurement. Communication from the Commission to the European Parliament, the Council, the European Economic and Social Committee and the Committee of Regions, European Commission, COM (2013) 455 Final, 25 June 2013

8. EC: Guide for the procurement of standards-based ICT - Elements of Good Practice. Communication from the Commission to the European Parliament, the Council, the European Economic and Social Committee and the Committee of Regions, European Commission, SWD (2013) 224 final, 25 June (Accompanying the document: 'Against lock-in: building open ICT systems by making better use of standards in public procurement', COM (2013) 455 final) (2013)

9. EC: Commission Recommendation (EU) 2017/1805 of 3 October 2017 on the professionalisation of public procurement - Building an architecture for the professionalisation of public procurement. Official Journal of the European Union, L259/28, 3 October 2017

10. EC: OPEN SOURCE SOFTWARE STRATEGY 2020 - 2023: Think Open. Communication to the Commission, European Commission, Communication, COM (2020) 7149 Final, 21 October 2020

11. Egyedi, T.: Standard-compliant, but incompatible?! Comput. Stand. Interfaces 29(6), 605–613 (2007)

12. EU: Online catalogue of ICT standard for procurement. European Commission, 6 November 2017. https://joinup.ec.europa.eu/community/european_catalogue. Accessed 6 Nov 2017

13. eSam: Checklista inför beslut om molntjänster i offentlig sektor, 31 October 2018. https://www.esamverka.se/stod-och-vagledning/rekommendationer-och-checklistor/checklista-infor-beslut-om-molntjanster-i-offenlig-sektor.html

14. eSam: Rättsligt uttalande om röjande och molntjänster, VER 2018:57, eSam, 23 October 2018

15. eSam (2021). www.esamverka.se/om-esam/om-esam.html

16. Farrell, J., Klemperer, P.: Coordination and lock-in: competition with switching costs and network effects. In: Armstrong, M., Porter, R. (eds.) Handbook of Industrial Organization, vol. 3, pp. 1967–2072. Elsevier, Berkeley (2007)

17. FLOSS: Open Source Software in the Public Sector: Policy within the European Union. FLOSS Final Report - Part 2b, Free/Libre Open Source Software: Survey and Study, Berlecon Research, Berlin, June 2002

18. Furberg, P., Westberg, M.: Måste myndigheter följa lagarna? Om utkontraktering och legalitet i digital miljö, Juridisk tidskrift, No. 2, pp. 406–417 (2020/21)

19. GAIA: Project GAIA-X: A Federated Data Infrastructure as the Cradle of a Vibrant European Ecosystem. Federal Ministry for Economic Affairs and Energy (BMWi), Berlin, October 2019. https://www.bmwi.de/Redaktion/EN/Publikationen/Digitale-Welt/project-gaia-x.html

20. GAIA: GAIA-X: Technical Architecture, Release - June 2020, Federal Ministry for Economic Affairs and Energy (BMWi), Berlin, June 2020. https://www.bmwi.de/Redaktion/EN/Publikationen/gaia-x-technical-architecture.pdf?__blob=publicationFile&v=5

21. Ghosh, R.A.: Open Standards and Interoperability Report: An Economic Basis for Open Standards, Deliverable D4. University of Maastricht, MERIT (2005)

22. Hon, W.K., Millard, C., Walden, I.: Negotiating cloud contracts: looking at clouds from both sides now. Stanford Technol. Law Rev. 16(1), 79–129 (2012)

23. Katz, A.: Google, APIs and the law. Use, reuse and lock-in. In: Lopez-Tarruella, A. (ed.) Google and the Law: Empirical Approaches to Legal Aspects of Knowledge-Economy Business Models, pp. 287–301. T.M.C. Asser Press, The Hague (2012), ISBN 978-90-6704-845-3

24. Lings, B., Lundell, B.: On the adaptation of grounded theory procedures: insights from the evolution of the 2G method. Inf. Technol. People 18(3), 196–211 (2005)

25. Lundell, B.: e-Governance in public sector ICT procurement: what is shaping practice in Sweden? Eur. J. ePract. 12(6), 66–78 (2011). http://web.archive.org/web/20110429011729/http://www.epractice.eu/files/European%20Journal%20epractice%20Volume%2012_6.pdf

26. Lundell, B., Gamalielsson, J., Katz, A.: On implementation of open standards in software: to what extent can ISO standards be implemented in open source software? Int. J. Stand. Res. **13**(1), 47–73 (2015)
27. Lundell, B., Gamalielsson, J., Katz, A.: Implementing IT standards in software: challenges and recommendations for organisations planning software development covering IT standards. Eur. J. Law Technol. **10**(2) (2019). https://ejlt.org/index.php/ejlt/article/view/709/
28. Lundell, B., Gamalielsson, J., Katz, A.: Addressing lock-in effects in the public sector: how can organisations deploy a SaaS solution while maintaining control of their digital assets? In: Virkar, S., et al. (ed.) CEUR Workshop Proceedings: EGOV-CeDEM-ePart 2020, vol. 2797, pp. 289–296, ISSN 1613-0073 (2020). http://ceur-ws.org/Vol-2797/paper28.pdf
29. Lundell, B., Gamalielsson, J., Tengblad, S.: IT-standarder, inlåsning och konkurrens: En analys av policy och praktik inom svensk förvaltning, Uppdragsforskningsrapport 2016:2, Konkurrensverket (the Swedish Competition Authority), ISSN: 1652-8089, (in Swedish, with an executive summary in English) (2016)
30. Lundell, B., et al.: Addressing lock-in, interoperability, and long-term maintenance challenges through open source: how can companies strategically use open source? In: Balaguer, et al. (eds.) The 13th International Conference on Open Source Systems (OSS 2017), IFIP AICT, vol. 496, pp. 80–88. Springer (2017)
31. NOC: The Netherlands in Open Connection: An Action Plan for the Use of Open Standards and Open Source Software in the Public and Semi-Public Sector. The Ministry of Economic Affairs, The Hague (2007)
32. NPS: Open IT-Standards. National Procurement Services, Kammarkollegiet, 7 March, Dnr 96-38-2014 (2016). https://www.avropa.se/globalassets/dokument/open-it-standards.pdf
33. NPS: Förstudierapport Webbaserat kontorsstöd, National Procurement Services, Kammarkollegiet, Dnr 23.2-6283-18, 22 February (in Swedish, with a summary in English) (2019). https://www.avropa.se/globalassets/forstudierapporter-vt--it/forstudierapport-webbaserat-kontorsstod2.pdf
34. UK: Open Standards Principles: For Software Interoperability, Data and Document Formats in Government IT Specifications. HM Government, 7 September 2012. https://assets.publishing.service.gov.uk/government/uploads/system/uploads/attachment_data/file/459074/Open-Standards-Principles-2012.pdf
35. UK: Open Standards Principles, GOV.UK, 7 September 2015. https://www.gov.uk/government/uploads/system/uploads/attachment_data/file/459075/OpenStandardsPrinciples2015.pdf
36. UK: Open Standards Principles, UK.GOV, 5 April 2018. https://assets.publishing.service.gov.uk/government/uploads/system/uploads/attachment_data/file/697195/Open_Standards_Principles_2018.odt

Finding Code-Clone Snippets in Large Source-Code Collection by ccgrep

Katsuro Inoue[1]([✉]), Yuya Miyamoto[1], Daniel M. German[2], and Takashi Ishio[3]

[1] Osaka University, Osaka, Japan
{inoue,yuy-mymt}@ist.osaka-u.ac.jp
[2] University of Victoria, Victoria, Canada
dmg@uvic.ca
[3] Nara Institute of Science and Technology, Ikoma-shi, Japan
ishio@is.naist.jp

Abstract. Finding the same or similar code snippets in the source code for a query code snippet is one of the fundamental activities in software maintenance. Code clone detectors detect the same or similar code snippets, but they report all of the code clone pairs in the target, which are generally excessive to the users. In this paper, we propose ccgrep, a token-based pattern matching tool with the notion of code clone pairs. The user simply inputs a code snippet as a query and specifies the target source code, and gets the matched code snippets as the result. The query and the result snippets form clone pairs. The use of special tokens (named meta-tokens) in the query allows the user to have precise control over the matching. It works for the source code in C, C++, Java, and Python on Windows or Unix with practical scalability and performance. The evaluation results show that ccgrep is effective in finding intended code snippets in large Open Source Software.

Keywords: Code snippet search · Pattern matching · Clone types

1 Introduction

Finding and locating the same or similar code snippets in source code files is a fundamental activity in software development and maintenance, and various kinds of software engineering tools or IDEs have been proposed and implemented [19].

A (code) clone is a code snippet that has an identical or similar snippet, and a pair of such snippets is called a (code) clone pair [6]. A large body of scientific literature on clone detection has been published and various kinds of code clone detection tools (detectors) have been developed [18,20]. These code clone detectors are candidates for finding similar code snippets, but most of those are designed to detect all of the code clone pairs in the target, which are generally excessive to the user who wants to search for a specific query snippet.

It has been reported that grep [8], a character-based pattern matching tool, is widely used in the software engineering practice to find lines with a specific

© IFIP International Federation for Information Processing 2021
Published by Springer Nature Switzerland AG 2021
D. Taibi et al. (Eds.): OSS 2021, IFIP AICT 624, pp. 28–41, 2021.
https://doi.org/10.1007/978-3-030-75251-4_3

keyword [14, 21], although making a query for a code snippet that spans multiple lines needs some skill and effort.

In this paper we propose a tool, named `ccgrep` (*code clone grep*), to find code snippets by using the notion of clone detection and pattern matching. Search queries can be simply code snippets, or code snippets enhanced with meta-tokens having a leading $ that can provide flexibility to narrow or broaden the search query. `ccgrep` is not an ordinary code clone detector that finds all code clone pairs in the target program but it is a code snippet finder that reports code snippets composing code clone pairs against the query snippet.

`ccgrep` works on Windows or Unix as a simple but reliable clone detector and pattern matching tool for C, C++, Java, and Python. `ccgrep` has been applied to various applications, and it showed high scalability and performance for large source-code collection. `ccgrep` is an Open Source Software system and can be obtained from GitHub[1].

2   Motivating Example

Some uses of the ternary operator (e.g., `exp1 ? exp2 : exp3` meaning the result of this entire expression is `exp2` if `exp1` is true, otherwise the result is `exp3`— available in C, C++ and Java) are considered bad practice [23]. For example, the use of `a< b ? a : b` is arguably harder to read than using `min(a,b)`. Therefore, it might be desirable to replace the ternary operator with a function or macro that returns the minimum value. The following is an example found in the file `drivers/usb/misc/adutux.c` in the Linux kernel (v5.2.0).

```
amount = bytes_to_read < data_in_secondary ?

                              bytes_to_read : data_in_secondary;
```

This line of code should be replaced with a more readable expression (note that the macro `min` in Linux guarantees no side effects):

```
amount = min(bytes_to_read, data_in_secondary);
```

We might consider that finding all occurrences of such usage of the ternary operator could be done by clone detectors. A popular clone detector NiCad [7] reports 646 block-level clone classes for the `drivers/usb` files by the default setting, but no snippet with the ternary operator case is included in the result because it is too small to be detectable.

Alternatively, we would try it with `grep` but it is not easy. For example, simply executing "`grep '<'`" for all 598 files (total 51,6394 lines in C) under `drivers/usb` produces 16335 matching, including many undesired patterns such as "`if (a<b)`", "`for (i=0; i<x; ...)`", or "`#include <linux/...>`". We could narrow the matches by concatenating `grep` like,

---

[1] https://github.com/yuy-m/CCGrep.

```
grep '<' -r . | grep '?' | grep ':'
```

However, it still produces 149 matches. Perhaps more problematic is that the expressions could span multiple lines. While it is possible to create a complex regular expression to find these expressions, it would be time-consuming and potentially error-prone.

Ideally, we would like to be able to specify a simple and easy-to-create-and-understand query to find these types of snippets. Therefore in this paper, we propose ccgrep and its query is written simply as:

```
a< b ? a : b
```

In a nutshell, this query specifies that a variable (represented by a) should be followed by < and then the second variable (represented by b), followed by a ?, followed by the same first variable found, followed by :, followed by the second variable. Also, white spaces and comments should be ignored. This query would match all type 2 clones (mentioned in Sect. 3.3) with consistent variable names such as x<y?x:y but it would not match x<y?x:z.

As a practical application, we have used this query to identify 3 instances of such an expression in Linux's drivers/usb and submitted patches to replace them with min. Two of those patches have been accepted already into Linux.

3   Overview of Code Clone Query by ccgrep

3.1   Basic Features

The input of ccgrep is the query and the target of the source code files in the same programming language. The output is a list of the matched code snippets in the target. The query and the matched code snippets form clone pairs. The query is a code snippet of single or multiple lines and is composed of the regular tokens in the language and the extended tokes with meta symbols having a leading $. We will describe these based on the classification of the clone types. Formalization of the matching is presented in Appendix and also in [11].

3.2   Query for Type 1 Clone

A Type 1 code clone pair is two code snippets possibly with different spacing, line break, or comment. To find type 1 cloned snippets, a code snippet in the programming language is directly given as the query, with a leading $ for each identifier or literal. Note that in the following examples, we will use Java as the programming language.

Query: `int $a= $0;`

Target: `int a=0 /* some comments */;`   *Match*

Target: `int b=0 ;`   *Not Match*

In this case, the query matches a code snippet with a comment, but it does not match the latter case of identifier b. The users do not worry about the white spaces and comments in the query.

3.3   Query for Type 2 Clone

A Type 2 code clone pair is two code snippets with the difference of the replacement of identifiers and literals, in addition to the difference of type 1 clones.

In type 2 matching, a user-defined identifier in the query matches any identifier in the target. The same also applies to literal. This "normalization" of the user-defined names allows very flexible pattern matching to find different identifiers or literals. By default, ccgrep executes so-called *Parameterized match* [3] or *P-match* for short, such that if two identifiers (or literals) in the query are the same, then the corresponding tokens in the target must be consistently the same. These normalization and p-match are formally explained in Appendix.

Query: `a = 0; a = a + b;`
Target: `y = 0; y = y + c;`   *Match*

Target: `y = 0; y = z + c;`   *Not Match*

In the former case, a consistently corresponds to y, but in the latter case, it does not[2].

3.4   Query for Type 3 Clone

A Type 3 code clone pair is two code snippets with a difference of some statements of addition, deletion, or change, in addition to the distinction of type 2. We employ wild-card tokens in the query, which extend the matching from the original seed tokens. The seed snippet and the matched snippet form a code clone pair of type 3. We can replace a token in the seed snippet with '$.' that matches any single token.

Seed: `a = 5 ;`
Query: `a = $. ;`
Target: `a = b ;`   *Match*

'$$' is a wild-card token to match zero or more tokens before the next token matches.

Seed: `a = 10 ;`
Query: `a = $$ ;`
Target: `a = b+c+10 ;`   *Match*
Target: `a = f(g,h) ;`   *Match*

The following is a more complex example.

Seed: `a= f(q); if(a<0){a=-a;}`

---

[2] This can be changed by an option to allow inconsistent matching.

Query: `a= $f(p); $$ if(a<0){a=-a;}`

Target: `b= f(q); if(b<0){b=-b;}`   *Match*

Target: `b= f(q); c= c+10; d=20; if(b<0){b=-b;}`   *Match*

3.5   Finding Various Code Snippets

Combining the regular tokens and meta-tokens in the query, we can find many different kinds of code patterns in the target, from simple to complex ones.

Method *XYZ* with no parameter
Query: `$XYZ( )`

Method *XYZ* with 0 or more parameters
Query: `$XYZ($$)`

Method *print* with variable *buf* as the 1st parameter
Query: `$print($buf, $$)`

Any method definition
Query: `T f($$){$$}`
   Note that type names are treated as identifiers and then T matches any type name.

Getter method
Query: `T f(){return this.v;}`

Setter method
Query: `T1 f(T2 v1){this.v1=v2;}`

***if* statement**
Query: `if ($$){$$}`

***for* statement using control variable**
Query: `for(T i=0; i<$$; i++){$$}`

In addition to finding these patterns, one of the usable use-cases would be a copy-and-paste code search. A developer finds a bug in a system and locates the snippet that causes the defects. She would want to find the same or similar occurrences of the bug in the system, then she copies the buggy snippet and runs `ccgrep` with the pasted snippet as the query. Then she instantly gets type 2 clone snippets. She does not need to set up a heavy clone detector, nor does she need to do tedious analysis of the unnecessary detection results.

4   Architecture of ccgrep

The architecture of `ccgrep` is presented in Fig. 1.

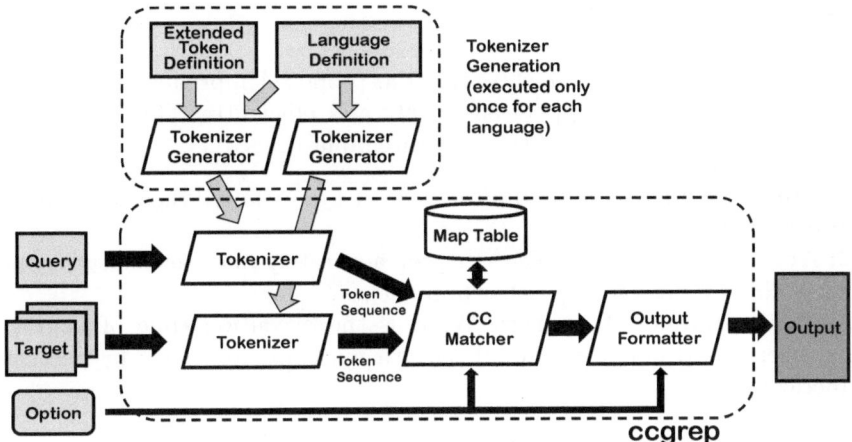

Fig. 1. Architecture of ccgrep

Tokenizer Generators: Parser generator ANTLR is used to generate two kinds of tokenizers. For the target tokenization, only the language definition is used to recognize the regular tokens, but for the query tokenization, the definition of the meta-tokens and that of regular tokens are used. This process has been executed only once for each target language.

Tokenizers: Each tokenizer removes white spaces and comments from the input files and decomposes the code into tokens. The query tokenizer accepts the meta-tokens starting with $ and the regular tokens defined by the language, but the target tokenizer accepts only the regular tokens. The tokenizer for the target files is executed in parallel for each file, along with the following CC Matcher.

CC Matcher: This performs a naive sequential pattern matching algorithm between two token sequences for the query (of the length m) and the target (of the length n), whose worst-case time complexity is $O(mn)$ [9]. For type 2 code clone matching, we record the position for each identifier and literal in Map Table to check proper P-matching. The table contents are flushed for each query. Option controls the normalization level, input language, output form, and many others.

Output Formatter: This process constructs the output for the successful matching result. Based on the input option, we can view the match result, like `grep`, in the form of the file name associated with the matched top line as the default, or as many other styles such as full matched lines, only the number of lines, or so on.

`ccgrep` is written in Java associated with the ANTLR output, and it is very easily installed and executed on various Unix or Windows environments with a single JAR file (about 1M byte) containing all necessary libraries.

5 Evaluation

The goal of the evaluation is to show that our proposed approach can find various kinds of intended code snippets effectively and efficiently. This goal could be decomposed into the following three research questions.

RQ1: Query Expressiveness. Are queries for various types of code clones expressible by `ccgrep`?

RQ2: Accuracy of ccgrep. Does `ccgrep` accurately find various types of code clones already detected by other approaches?

RQ3: Performance of ccgrep. What is the execution time of `ccgrep`? Is the token-based naive sequential pattern matching approach fast enough in practice?

5.1 RQ1: Query Expressiveness

As shown in previous sections, it is obvious that our approach can easily create various query patterns for type 1 matching, type 2 matching with P-match, and type 2 matching with non-P-match, by specifying a code snippet associated with appropriate options. In addition, we can specify the name of an identifier or literal, if we place $ before the name.

A type 3 code-clone snippet is one with a few statement addition, or deletion, or change for a seed snippet. Thus the query for type 3 matching could be made from the seed by adding meta-tokens such as $., $$, or $*, deleting some regular tokens in the seed, or modifying some regular tokens with $., $$, or other meta-tokens.

Therefore, the queries for type 1 to 3 code clones can be effectively created from a code snippet at hand.

5.2 RQ2: Accuracy of ccgrep

For evaluation of query-matching (or information retrieval) systems, recall and precision values, computed by comparing the matched results with the oracles for the queries, are popularly employed [2]. Here in our approach, however, the query to CC matching has no ambiguity and it reports the matching result rigorously as expected and specified by the query with options. In such a sense, the result is always the same as the oracle, i.e., the recall and precision are always 1. Thus, instead of using recall and precision, here we simply investigate if `ccgrep` works accurately in the sense that code clones already reported by other approaches could be found by our approach.

For this purpose, first, we have employed BigCloneBench [24] which is a huge collection of various kinds of code clones. We have extracted all pairs classified as type 1 and type 2 code clones from BigCloneBench, and for each clone pair ($sp1, sp2$), we have checked if $sp2$ is successfully found in the result of `ccgrep` for $sp1$ as a query with appropriate options, and vice versa. Table 1 shows the numbers of type 1 and 2 clones found by `ccgrep`.

Table 1. Checked clones in BigCloneBench

Clone type	Clone pairs	Found	Not found
Type 1	48116	48111	5
Type 2	4234	4232	2
Total	52350	52343	7

As we can see in Table 1, most type 1 and 2 clones are found accurately. There were several cases of not-found clones, and we have investigated further those cases and recognized that those cases are faults of the classification of BigCloneBench, some of which should be classified into type 3, and some others are not clones. Thus, we can say that all of the proper type 1 and 2 clones in BigCloneBench were perfectly found by `ccgrep`.

For type 3 clones, since BigCloneBench contains huge type 3 data and we cannot make the queries for those, we have instead used CBCD data [16], that contains 11 type-3 clone sets taken from the source code of Git, the Linux kernel, and PostgreSQL. We have crafted type 3 queries from one of the code snippets in each clone set as the seed and have checked if those queries accurately match the other snippets in the same clone set. We have confirmed that all the crafted queries accurately match other snippets in each clone set.

As far as our investigation, all the matches are controlled by the query and are performed accurately as we have expected.

5.3   RQ3: Performance of ccgrep

It is interesting to know that our approach, i.e., token-based and naive sequential pattern matching, can be implemented fast enough for practical use. We have examined various queries for `ccgrep` with the target source files of Antlr and Ant in Java, and CBCD data (Git, PostgreSQL, and Linux Kernel) in C, and have measured the performance of `ccgrep`. Following are employed queries. All execution was made with the default setting of `ccgrep` except for the language option.

qA: `a < b? a: b`
   Find ternary operation to give a smaller value.
qB: `T1 f(T2 a) { return $$; }`
   Find function definition immediately returning a value.
qC: `f($$, $$, $$);`
   Find three parameter function.

qD:
```
for(a = 0; a < $$; a++) { $$ }      $|
a = 0; while(a < $$) { $$ a++; }
```

Find **for** or (represented by **$|**) **while** statement with a control variable.

Table 2. Target and execution result by **ccgrep**

Target		Antlr	Ant	Git	PgSQL	Linux
Lang.		Java	Java	C	C	C
#file		678	1,272	339	904	15,123
#line		59,511	138,396	90,495	177,174	3,756,212
qA	#found	0	2	8	3	48
	time (sec.)	**1.12**	**1.32**	**1.11**	**1.43**	**9.46**
qB	#found	159	161	7	27	543
	time (sec.)	**1.15**	**1.33**	**1.10**	**1.47**	**10.15**
qC	#found	1,710	2,487	5,717	10,603	187,653
	time (sec.)	**1.20**	**1.38**	**1.13**	**1.55**	**12.01**
qD	#found	1	13	442	621	10,754
	time (sec.)	**1.19**	**1.52**	**1.10**	**1.49**	**11.06**

Antlr: Antlr4 v.4.7.2, Ant: Apache Ant v.1.10.5, Git: v.1.6.4.3,
PgSQL: PostgreSQL v.6.5.3, Linux: Linux kernel v.2.6.14rc2

Table 2 shows the size metrics of the target, the number of found snippets, and the execution time of each query on a workstation with Intel Xeon E5-1603v4 (@2.8 GHz × 4), 32 GB RAM, and Windows 10 Pro for WS 64bit.

As we can see from Table 2, the execution times are about 1–10 s even for a few million lines of Linux kernel target. We would think that those are fast and acceptable as a daily-use tool. The execution times for qA to qD are very stable for each target. For example, in the case of Linux, they are about 10 s. even for the small #found case (48 for qA) and the large #found case (187,653 for qC). Thus, we would say that the execution time is not heavily affected by the result size (#found) but mainly affected by the target size (#line). Targets Ant in Java and PgSQL in C have similar sizes around 140–180 Klines, and the execution times are also similar around 1–1.5 s. This would show that the execution time is not strongly affected by the target language.

For comparison to **grep** we have employed a query qE, that is almost equivalent to qA except qE does not match the targets with more than one line.

qE(grep):
```
([a-zA-Z_][a-zA-Z_0-9]*)\s*<
([a-zA-Z_][a-zA-Z_0-9]*)\s*\?\s*
\1\s*:\s*\2
```

This query is complex and hard to create for inexperienced **grep** users. It has been executed by **grep** 3 to 9 times faster than **ccgrep**, but it missed some expected matches of the code snippets with two or more lines.

As the conclusion of RQ3, although the speed of `ccgrep` is slower than `grep`, it is sufficiently fast and acceptable as a search tool even for large targets such as 3 million LOC Linux kernel.

6   Related Works

There are numerous publications on code clone detection methods and their tools [18,20]. Most of those tools focus on finding all of the code clone pairs in the target file collection. They report all code clones or similar code snippets with similarities higher than a certain threshold. Precisely controlling the matches with meta-symbols like ours cannot be accomplished by those approaches.

There are several tools specialized for finding code snippets. CBCD has been designed for finding related code snippets from a buggy code snippet, by using matching of Program Dependence Graph (PDG) [16]. It can be used to find type 1, 2, and 3 clones; however, the matching generally requires a long pre-processing time to construct PDG, and so this approach would not fit the nimble clone finding that we are interested in. NCDSearch has been designed to find similar code snippets in the pile of source code files for the analysis of code reuse and evolution [12]. The approach would be unique and interesting, but the speed is slower than ours. Micro-clones are recently getting focus due to their importance [4,13]. Our tool is one of the convenience tools for finding micro clones.

Siamese has been developed for finding code clone pairs for a query method or file using multiple representations of n-gram token sequences with inverted index [17]. It requires a long indexing time (e.g., about 10 min indexing time for 10,000 method target). Thus its application and usage would be different from ours.

Variants of `grep` such as context grep `cgrep`, approximate grep `agrep`, and many others had been proposed and implemented to meet various requirements [1]. However, there is no one for clone-based matching like ours. Semantic-based matching tool `sgrep` [5], data-structure-based matching tool `coccigrep` [15], and the logic-based query pattern capturing language [22] were proposed, where the specific notations for the queries are provided without using the notion of clones like ours.

7   Conclusions

We have presented `ccgrep` that effectively finds code snippets in the target files with the notion of code clone and meta-pattern. It is a practical and effective pattern matching tool, easy-to-use to many software engineers.

As a future direction, we are interested in further performance improvement by using more efficient pattern matching algorithms. Also, we are trying to spread the use of `ccgrep` to industry collaborators who are trying to detect similar bug patterns in their legacy systems.

Acknowledgments. This work was partially supported by JSPS KAKENHI Grant Number 18H04094, and Osaka University Program for Promoting International Joint Research. We are grateful for important comments from T. Kamiya, N. Yoshida, Raula Gaikovina Kula, E. Choi, K. Takenouchi, T. Kanda, and M. Matsushita.

Table 3. Token-level matching

Token(s) in query	Matched token(s) in target	Simple example of match	
		Query	Target
Reserved word†	Exact reserved word	`while`	`while`
Delimiter	Exact delimiter	`(`	`(`
Identifier	Any identifier‡	`myname`	`abc`
Literal	Any literal‡	`1`	`100`
$identifier	Exact identifier	`$myname`	`myname`
$literal	Exact literal	`$1`	`1`
$.	Any single token	`$.`	`if`
$# X	Any shortest token sequence ending with X	`$# +`	`while(f(a+`
$$ X	Any shortest token sequence ending with X, excluding X inside well-balanced bracket {...}, [...], or (...)	`$$ +`	`while(f(a+1))+`
X $— Y	Either X or Y	`+ $| -`	`-`
X $*	Repeated sequence of X zero or more times	`( $*`	`(((`
X $+	Repeated sequence of X one or more times	`( $+`	`((`
X $?	X or none	`( $?`	`(`
$(X1 X2 ... $)	X1, X2, ... (group for further regular expression operations)	`$( a++ $| ++a $)`	`a++`

†Type names are treated as identifiers.
‡Identifier and literal may match only the exact one by an option.
- Tokens starting with $ are meta-tokens and others are regular tokens.
- Wildcard meta-tokens $# and $$ match in reluctant way, and $*, $+, and $? match in possessive way [10].
- X, Y, X1, X2, ... are any regular token or a group with $(... $).

Appendix: Formulating Matching

Here we formulate the matching made by ccgrep. The input of the matching is the query q, the target T of source code files in a programming language L, and matching option o. The output is a list of matched code snippet t in T. We refer to reserved words, delimiters (operators, brackets, ; ...), identifiers, and literals in L as *regular tokens*. Other tokens starting with meta symbol $ are called *meta-tokens*. q is a sequence of regular tokens and the meta-tokes, and each matched result t is a sequence of the regular tokens. These token sequences do not contain comments, white spaces, or line breaks. We always consider the matching on the token sequence level, not on the character level.

In Table 3, we define a token-level matching for various kinds of tokens with simple examples. The basic ideas of these matches are as follows.

- A language-defined token such as reserved words or delimiters matches the exact token.
- A user-defined token such as an identifier or literal can match the same kind of token with a possibly different name or value. To pin down them to a specific identifier name or literal value, $ is used before the token. For example, $count would match only the token count.
- Wildcard tokens $., $#, and $$ are introduced for the matches to any single token, any token sequence, or any token sequence discarding paired brackets, respectively.
- Popular regular expression operators for choice, repetition, and grouping are introduced to enhance the expressiveness.

Consider that query q is a token sequence $q_1, ..., q_m$ $(1 \leq m)$, and a target t is a token sequence $t_1, ..., t_n$ $(0 \leq n)$. From q_1 to q_m, if each token in the query matches tokens in the target from t_1 to t_n as defined in Table 3 without overlapping or orphan tokens, then we say q matches t.

For the query token sequence $q_1, ..., q_m$ and the target token sequence $t_1, ..., t_n$, if $n = m$ and $norm(q_i) = norm(t_i)$ for each i, then q matches t as *type 2 matching*. Here $norm$ is a normalization function to flat the distinction of identifiers (or literals), defined below.

$$norm(x) \equiv \begin{cases} \#id & \text{if } x \text{ is an identifier} \\ \#li & \text{if } x \text{ is an literal} \\ x & \text{otherwise} \end{cases}$$

In type 2 matching, an identifier in the query can match any identifier in the target, and also a literal in the query can match any literal in the target.

```
q1: a = 0;  b = 10;
t1: x = 10;  y = 200;
```

q1 matches t2, because the sequences of the normalized tokens are both $[\#id, =,$ $\#li, ;, \#id, =, \#li, ;]$.

A special case of type 2 matching, with a constraint such that for any identifier or literal q_i if $q_i = q_j$, then $t_i = t_j$, is *Parameterized matching* or *P-matching*. This is sometimes referred to consistent or aligned matching, meaning the same identifiers (or literals) in the query are mapped into the same ones in the target. P-matching is formally defined with a specialized normalization function $norm_p()$, as follows.

$$norm_p(x) \equiv \begin{cases} \#id_{pos(x)} & \text{if } x \text{ is an identifier} \\ \#li_{pos(x)} & \text{if } x \text{ is a literal} \\ x & \text{otherwise} \end{cases}$$

Here, $pos(x)$ is a function returning position i such that identifier (or literal) x is the i-th identifier (literal) newly appeared in the token sequence. Note that any meta-token starting with $ in the query and their matched tokens in the target are out of consideration of $pos()$.

q2: a = 0; a = a + b;
t2: y = 0; y = y + c;

For q2, $pos(a) = 1$ and $pos(b) = 2$, and for t2, $pos(y) = 1$ and $pos(c) = 2$. q2 matches t2 as P-matching, because the P-normalized sequences are both $[\#id_1, =, \#li_1, ;, \#id_1, =, \#id_1, +, \#id_2, ;]$. The following case is type 2 matching but not P-matching.

q3: a = 0; a = a + b;
t3: y = 0; y = z + c; (type 2 matching but not P-matching)

At t3, z cannot be matched by a because $norm_p(a) = \#id_1$ is not equal to $norm_p(z) = \#id_2$. As a default of CC matching, P-matching is assumed but it can be changed by the tool's option.

References

1. Abou-Assaleh, T., Ai, W.: Survey of global regular expression print (grep) tools (2004). http://citeseerx.ist.psu.edu/viewdoc/summary?doi=10.1.1.95.3326
2. Baeza-Yates, R., Ribeiro-Neto, B.: Modern Information Retrieval. ACM Press/Addison-Wesley, New York (1999)
3. Baker, B.S.: A program for identifying duplicated code. In: Proceedings of Computing Science and Statistics: 24th Symposium on the Interface, vol. 24, pp. 49–57 (1992)
4. Beller, M., Zaidman, A., Karpov, A., Zwaan, R.A.: The last line effect explained. Empir. Softw. Eng. **22**(3), 1508–1536 (2016). https://doi.org/10.1007/s10664-016-9489-6
5. Bull, R.I., Trevors, A., Malton, A.J., Godfrey, M.W.: Semantic grep: regular expressions + relational abstraction. In: 2002 Proceedings of the Ninth Working Conference on Reverse Engineering, pp. 267–276, November 2002. https://doi.org/10.1109/WCRE.2002.1173084
6. Carter, S., Frank, R., Tansley, D.: Clone detection in telecommunications software systems: a neural net approach. In: Proceedings of the International Workshop on Application of Neural Networks to Telecommunications, pp. 273–287 (1993)

7. Cordy, J.R., Roy, C.K.: The NiCad clone detector. In: 2011 IEEE 19th International Conference on Program Comprehension, pp. 219–220, June 2011. https://doi.org/10.1109/ICPC.2011.26
8. FreeSoftwareFoundation: Gnu grep 3.3 manual (2018). https://www.gnu.org/software/grep/manual/grep.html
9. Gusfield, D.: Algorithms on Strings, Trees and Sequences. Cambridge University Press, New York (1997)
10. Habibi, M.: Java Regular Expressions: Taming the Java.util.regex Engine. Apress (2004). https://doi.org/10.1007/978-1-4302-0709-2
11. Inoue, K., Miyamoto, Y., German, D.M., Ishio, T.: Code clone matching: a practical and effective approach to find code snippets. arXiv CS.SE(2003:05615v1), pp. 1–11 (2020)
12. Ishio, T., Maeda, N., Shibuya, K., Inoue, K.: Cloned buggy code detection in practice using normalized compression distance. In: 2018 IEEE International Conference on Software Maintenance and Evolution, ICSME 2018, Madrid, Spain, 23–29 September 2018, pp. 591–594 (2018)
13. Islam, J., Mondal, M., Roy, C., Schneider, K.: Comparing bug replication in regular and micro code clones. In: 27th International Conference on Program Comprehension (ICPC 2019), pp. 81–92, May 2019
14. Kernighan, B., Pike, B.: The Practice of Programming. Addison-Wesley, Boston (1999)
15. Leblond, E.: Coccigrep introduction. http://home.regit.org/software/coccigrep/
16. Li, J., Ernst, M.D.: CBCD: cloned buggy code detector. In: 2012 34th International Conference on Software Engineering (ICSE), pp. 310–320, June 2012. https://doi.org/10.1109/ICSE.2012.6227183
17. Ragkhitwetsagul, C., Krinke, J.: Siamese: scalable and incremental code clone search via multiple code representations. Empir. Softw. Eng. **24**(4), 2236–2284 (2019). https://doi.org/10.1007/s10664-019-09697-7
18. Rattan, D., Bhatia, R., Singh, M.: Software clone detection: a systematic review. Inf. Softw. Technol. **55**(7), 1165–1199 (2013)
19. Roehm, T., Tiarks, R., Koschke, R., Maalej, W.: How do professional developers comprehend software? In: Proceedings of the 34th International Conference on Software Engineering, ICSE 2012, pp. 255–265. IEEE Press, Piscataway (2012). http://dl.acm.org/citation.cfm?id=2337223.2337254
20. Roy, C.K., Cordy, J.R., Koschke, R.: Comparison and evaluation of code clone detection techniques and tools: a qualitative approach. Sci. Comput. Program. **74**(7), 470–495 (2009)
21. Singer, J., Lethbridge, T.C.: What's so great about 'grep'? Implications for program comprehension tools. Technical report, National Research Council, Canada (1997)
22. Sivaraman, A., Zhang, T., Van den Broeck, G., Kim, M.: Active inductive logic programming for code search. In: Proceedings of the 41st International Conference on Software Engineering, pp. 292–303. IEEE Press (2019)
23. Soetens, Q.D., Demeyer, S.: Studying the effect of refactorings: a complexity metrics perspective. In: 2010 Seventh International Conference on the Quality of Information and Communications Technology, pp. 313–318, September 2010. https://doi.org/10.1109/QUATIC.2010.58
24. Svajlenko, J., Roy, C.K.: Evaluating clone detection tools with BigCloneBench. In: 2015 IEEE International Conference on Software Maintenance and Evolution (ICSME), pp. 131–140. IEEE (2015)

OSS PESTO: An Open Source Software Project Evaluation and Selection TOol

Xiaozhou Li[(✉)] and Sergio Moreschini

Tampere University, Kalevantie 4, 33100 Tampere, Finland
{xiaozhou.li,sergio.moreschini}@tuni.fi

Abstract. Open source software (OSS), playing an increasingly critical role nowadays, has been commonly adopted and integrated in various software products. For many practitioners, selecting and adopting suitable OSS can help them greatly. Though many studies have been conducted on proposing OSS evaluation and selection models, a limited number are followed and used in the industry. Meanwhile, many existing OSS evaluation tools, though providing valuable details, fall short on offering intuitive suggestions in terms of framework-supported evaluation factors. Towards filling the gap, we propose an Open Source Software Project Evaluation and Selection TOol (OSS PESTO). Targeting OSS on Github, the largest OSS source code host, it facilitates the evaluation practice by enabling practitioners to compare candidates therein in terms of selected OSS evaluation models. It also allows in-time Github data collection and customized evaluation that enriches its effectiveness and ease of use.

Keywords: Open source software · Open source evaluation · Github mining

1 Introduction

During the last two decades, open source software (OSS) has been flourishing with such trend continuing [10] and nowadays, OSS is adopted by the vast majority of IT companies [12,13]. On Github, the largest OSS source code host, more than 60 million users[1] have participated in over 100 million open source projects[2], among which many have been widely adopted by users and companies. However, due to such a large number of candidates, for many practitioners, selecting a suitable OSS product or library is difficult, especially when the relevant information are not explicitly provided [12].

To support the OSS evaluation and selection practice, many studies provide models and frameworks as guidance [7,18,21,23,24]. During the last two decades, 35 models are proposed with checklists, measures or both provided [12]. They

---

[1] https://github.com/search?q=type:user&type=Users.
[2] https://github.com/search?q=is:public.

© IFIP International Federation for Information Processing 2021
Published by Springer Nature Switzerland AG 2021
D. Taibi et al. (Eds.): OSS 2021, IFIP AICT 624, pp. 42–50, 2021.
https://doi.org/10.1007/978-3-030-75251-4_4

all work similarly with a process of "candidate software identification - factor evaluation - scoring". In addition, many tools are designed and proposed to facilitate such practice [4,18,21,23]. However, many tools are rigidly designed and allow limited customization. Meanwhile, among those proposed, only two are properly maintained with the majority being not available any more [12].

As the largest OSS host and platform, Github is a valuable channel restoring and presenting OSS related information. Retrospective analysis of Github repositories, based on the abundant information on code, developers, organizations and activities within, can yield valuable insights into the evolution and growth of OSS and facilitate decision making processes [17]. Many studies have used such data source and conduct research on various OSS related perspectives [9,15,22]. However, the approaches towards using Github data for OSS evaluation are limited, let alone tools to support such practice.

Herein, we propose OSS PESTO, an open source tool facilitating OSS evaluation and selection. Comparatively, besides being fully open sourced and free to use, OSS PESTO has the following advantages: 1) it allows users to update in-time Github data; 2) it allows users to customize evaluation with models or preference; 3) it allows users to save data locally and to use it without network connection; 4) it is always accessible as maintained in Github repository. It shall largely help the practitioners to compare and evaluate OSS candidates freely, timely and efficiently.

The remainder of this paper is organized as follows. Section 2 introduces the related work on OSS evaluation tools. Section 3 presents OSS PESTO with details. Section 4 presents an experiment validating its applicability. Section 5 concludes the article.

2   Related Work

The Open Source Maturity Model (OSMM) is the first proposed model and open standard that aims for such purpose [7]. Guided by OSMM, the practitioners will evaluate OSS by its maturity of each aspect, weight each aspect with importance, and compute its overall maturity by the weighted sum. Compared to OSMM, the Open Business Readiness Rating (OpenBRR) is an OSS evaluation method with more indicators, the idea of target uses and the customized evaluation [24]. The method provides an index applicable to all OSS development initiatives. Its main limits are related to the incompatibility of the requirements between different targets and to the difficulty of choosing the proper reference application for some projects. Similarly, a number of evaluation models are proposed, for example, Qualification and Selection of Open Source Software (QSOS) [18], OpenBQR [21], OSSPAL [23], which provide enhanced guidance and methodological support.

QSOS tool is designed to support the QSOS model which aims to qualify, select and compare OSS products [18]. However, the rigidness of compulsory Identity Card setting and all criteria inclusion is commonly seen as its limitation. OpenQBR [21] requires specification on factor importance before the assessment of the project. Compared to the QSOS tool, OpenQBR is more elastics as not require to evaluate factors which are not relevant to the specific project.

OSS-PAL [23], though similar to QSOS, aims to partially automate the evaluation of the projects. Despite the appealing goal of the project, it fails to provide the automated data collection function. Other works investigated the availability of the information on online portals [14,20], but they did not provide tools for collecting or aggregating data.

In addition, many other tools are available over time but have been discontinued, including real-time OpenSSL execution monitoring system (ROSEN) [4], RAP TOOL [8], SQO-OSS [19], OMM Tool [5], T-Doc Tool [16], QualiPSo Trustworthiness Checklist [3], MOSST [6] and OP2A Checklist [1] and other checklist included in marketing models for OSS [2,11].

With OSS PESTO, we aim to overcome some of the most common drawbacks of all of these tools, such as, the focus on specific factors, the evaluation of factors before adding a weight function or the lack of control for both internal and external product quality.

3 OSS PESTO

We implement OSS PESTO[3] by following the commonly acknowledged OSS evaluation process summarized from previous studies [12]. It shall contain the following main activities: 1) identify the OSS candidates; 2) elicit a list of factors that need to be evaluated and the according metrics that measure such factors; 3) provide scores or selection recommendation as evaluation output.

In addition, in order to use the latest Github data to evaluate OSS, we integrate a data crawler module in OSS PESTO. It enables the users to crawl the required repository and activities information of any existing OSS projects. Additionally, it also allows them to crawl the data of a list of projects based on the selected range of stars. Furthermore, OSS PESTO allows users to customize evaluation factors based on the selection of models and/or their personal preferences.

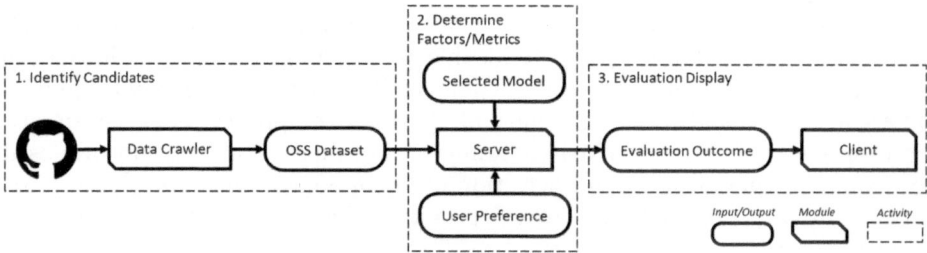

Fig. 1. OSS PESTO framework

---

[3] Source code: https://github.com/clowee/OSS-PESTO.

Shown in Fig. 1, OSS PESTO contains three individual modules as follows.

- **Data Crawler**: The data crawler module contains a set of Python scripts that extract Github repository data via Github APIs[4]. It enables the users to select the candidate OSS and extract the according data.
- **Server**: The server side is implemented by ReactJS[5] while database with MongoDB[6]. The evaluation model is described with the config.json file, which can be altered with users' preference of evaluation factors.
- **Client**: The client side is also implemented by ReactJS. It mainly displays the candidate OSS projects with the selected attributes/factors shown. It also shows the results of candidate comparison which facilitates OSS evaluation and selection.

Figure 1 also shows the activities of utilizing OSS PESTO to evaluate candidate OSS projects as follows.

- **Step 1**. identifies the OSS candidates by running the data crawler module to extract the according dataset.
- **Step 2**. select the evaluation model, configure evaluation preference, and run the server module.
- **Step 3**. run the client module and compare the OSS candidates by the selected factors.

The crawled data is saved locally in A comma-separated values (CSV) file with each row containing the values of an individual OSS candidate. To be noted, the required data can be selectively crawled according to the users, who determine which metrics are the important ones when evaluating particular aspects of OSS. Such selection of data can be guided by the evaluation model chosen by the evaluator. For example, when selecting only the most popular OSS, the numbers of stars, watches, and download are the ones to be crawled.

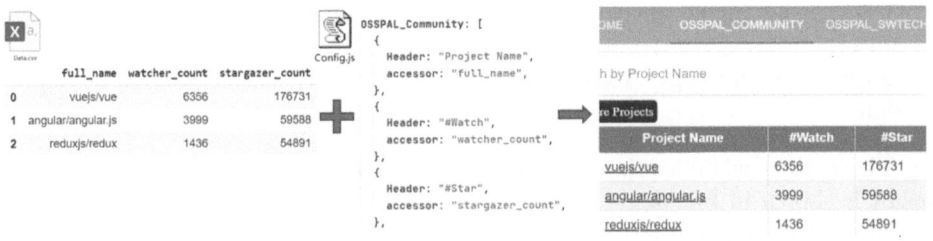

Fig. 2. An example of configuration file

Furthermore, the configuration file is a Javascript file mapping the category tabs displayed by the client and the data features/metrics that are selected to

---

[4] https://docs.github.com/en/graphql; https://docs.github.com/en/rest.

[5] https://reactjs.org/.

[6] https://www.mongodb.com/.

evaluate the according categories. Shown in 2 is an example of how a configuration file works. By editing the configuration file, the users can customize their selection of metrics, the evaluation categories and the links in between. For example, if the user chooses to focus on the popularity of OSS and uses the number of watches as the metric for it, the according piece of code {*Header: "#Watch", accessor: "watcher_count"*} shall be added to the "Popularity" tab block.

4   Experiment Showcase

In order to validate the applicability of OSS PESTO, we conduct a series of experiments, including the testing of all three modules. The testing scenario is to evaluate and compare three JavaScript frameworks, i.e., Angular[7], Redux[8] and Vue[9] using the OSSPAL model [23]. The evaluation categories include "Community", "Support", "Operational Software Characteristics", "Documentation", "Software Technology Attributes", "Functionality" and "Development Process". Herein, we focus on the "Community", "Support" and "Software Technology Attributes" aspects, which can be well demonstrated by the obtained data.

To start crawling the Github data, given the user's Github personal token and the target OSS candidates as input, the data crawler module can be ran individually and continuously. Towards the stated objective, the crawling process takes within two minutes. When the data is ready, we prepare the config.json by selecting the target metrics that are valuable towards evaluating each factors of the candidates. For each of the selected factors, the according metrics are as follows.

- Community: number of watches, number of stars, age, average issue active time, average issue comments, number of pull requests, and number of issue raiser.
- Support: average issue closed time, number of contributor, organization issue raiser.
- Software Technology Attributes: number of open issues, number of dependence.

Thereafter, when running both the server and the client, the comparison result is shown in Fig. 3.

Based on such comparison, we can easily observe that despite not being the oldest community, Vue is more popular than the other two candidates in terms of watches and stars. However, these three communities are active in different ways, as Angular has more comments on issues, pull requests, and different issue raisers while the others are more responsive to issues (shown in Fig. 3(a)). Regarding support, Angular has a much larger contributor group and organizational issue

---

[7] https://angular.io/.

[8] https://redux.js.org/.

[9] https://vuejs.org/.

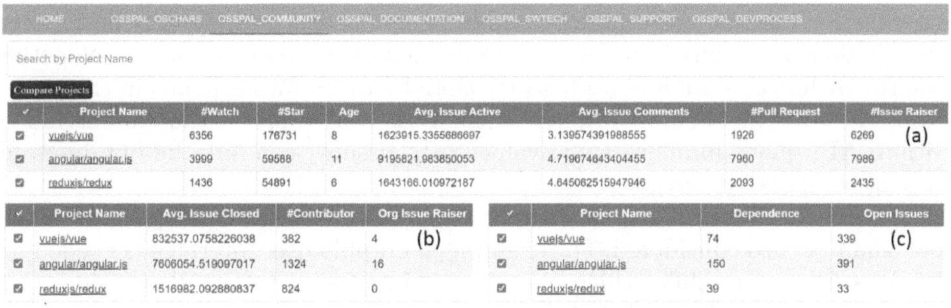

✓	Project Name	#Watch	#Star	Age	Avg. Issue Active	Avg. Issue Comments	#Pull Request	#Issue Raiser
☑	vuejs/vue	6356	176731	8	1623915.3355686697	3.139574391988555	1926	6269
☑	angular/angular.js	3999	59588	11	9195821.983850053	4.719674643404455	7960	7989
☑	reduxjs/redux	1436	54891	6	1643166.010972187	4.645062515947946	2093	2435

✓	Project Name	Avg. Issue Closed	#Contributor	Org Issue Raiser
☑	vuejs/vue	832537.0758226038	382	4
☑	angular/angular.js	7606054.519097017	1324	16
☑	reduxjs/redux	1516982.092880837	824	0

✓	Project Name	Dependence	Open Issues
☑	vuejs/vue	74	339
☑	angular/angular.js	150	391
☑	reduxjs/redux	39	33

Fig. 3. Experiment results demonstration

raiser for support, while on software technology attribute aspect, Redux has much less dependence and open issues (shown in Fig. 3(b) and (c)).

When adopting a different evaluation model, it is possible that by taking into account particular overseen metrics, the user obtains new insights regarding the selected candidates. For example, the SQO-OSS model [19] sees "Growth in active developers" as a metric to evaluate the "Developer base" category, when OSSPAL has not such category. However, due to the fact that same dataset is used for all potential models, it is hardly possible to have opposite comparative evaluation result for the same category from different models.

5 Conclusion

This paper presents OSS PESTO, an open source software project evaluation and selection tool, to support the practitioners' need towards OSS evaluation and selection. This tool provides a Github-repository-data-oriented, easy-to-maintain, customization-friendly solution. It shall benefit the practitioners in both industry and academia in terms of the different focuses on either the OSS projects or the OSS evaluation models respectively.

However, the current version of this tool can certainly be improved in the following ways. Firstly, OSS PESTO has not yet supported the practitioners' selection of OSS candidates at the identification phase in terms of their target functionalities. As the accessible data obtained from Github does not provide explicit information regarding the main features of the OSS, such candidate selection cannot be automated via direct identification. A potential solution is to apply natural language processing (NLP) techniques to identify and summarize such main features from the description and Readme text of the projects. Such a feature shall be implemented in our future work.

Furthermore, the current version only utilizes limited amount of the attributes provided by the Github API. For many such attributes, the explicit mappings towards particular OSS evaluation categories are not verified. For example, the number of OSS downloads can be seen as a metric for its popularity. However, unless a particular user insists it being a critical evaluation criterion for his/her customized evaluation model, such value can be ignored when it does not contribute to any pre-defined evaluation categories. Nonetheless, the inclusion of more data features shall be taken into account in the future work. However, it should be noted such work can result in the exhaustion of Github API query limit, as some values (e.g., issues) can only be obtained via looping enumerated results.

In addition, more features, in terms of the ease of use perspective of the tool, shall be also considered. For example, a graphic user interface is needed for the data crawler module which can also be integrated to the server side. Furthermore, the data from Github has its limitation on reflecting certain aspects of OSS. For example, the development process of the projects cannot be easily accessed externally, except for the number of releases and the release pace. Thus, in order to improve the potential scope of this tool, more data sources are required with more techniques required to process possibly unstructured data as well. Meanwhile, more practical features, such as, exporting the evaluation results, adding weight to different factors, editor of configure files, and model customization interface, are also required.

Our future work shall focus on integrating the modules and enhancing the overall quality of the tool according to the above mentioned limitation. It is also important to investigate the ways of evaluating individual OSS by providing unified quantified results. In addition, we shall systematically investigate the availability of data from multiple sources that could be used to support OSS evaluation.

References

1. Benlian, A., Hess, T.: Comparing the relative importance of evaluation criteria in proprietary and open-source enterprise application software selection-a conjoint study of ERP and office systems. Inf. Syst. J. **21**(6), 503–525 (2011)
2. del Bianco, V., Lavazza, L., Lenarduzzi, V., Morasca, S., Taibi, D., Tosi, D.: A study on OSS marketing and communication strategies. In: Hammouda, I., Lundell, B., Mikkonen, T., Scacchi, W. (eds.) OSS 2012. IAICT, vol. 378, pp. 338–343. Springer, Heidelberg (2012). https://doi.org/10.1007/978-3-642-33442-9_31
3. del Bianco, V., Lavazza, L., Morasca, S., Taibi, D., Tosi, D.: The QualiSPo approach to OSS product quality evaluation. In: Proceedings of the 3rd International Workshop on Emerging Trends in Free/Libre/Open Source Software Research and Development, pp. 23–28 (2010)
4. Choi, S., Kang, Y., Lee, G.: A security evaluation and testing methodology for open source software embedded information security system. In: Gervasi, O., et al. (eds.) ICCSA 2005. LNCS, vol. 3481, pp. 215–224. Springer, Heidelberg (2005). https://doi.org/10.1007/11424826_23
5. del Bianco, V., Lavazza, L., Morasca, S., Taibi, D.: Quality of open source software: the QualiPSo trustworthiness model. In: Boldyreff, C., Crowston, K., Lundell, B., Wasserman, A.I. (eds.) OSS 2009. IAICT, vol. 299, pp. 199–212. Springer, Heidelberg (2009). https://doi.org/10.1007/978-3-642-02032-2_18

6. Del Bianco, V., Lavazza, L., Morasca, S., Taibi, D., Tosi, D.: A survey on the importance of some economic factors in the adoption of open source software. In: Lee, R., Ormandjieva, O., Abran, A., Constantinides, C. (eds.) Software Engineering Research, Management and Applications 2010. Studies in Computational Intelligence, vol. 296, pp. 151–162. Springer, Heidelberg. https://doi.org/10.1007/978-3-642-13273-5_10

7. Duijnhouwer, F.W., Widdows, C.: Capgemini expert letter open source maturity model. Capgemini, 1–18 (2003)

8. Immonen, A., Palviainen, M.: Trustworthiness evaluation and testing of open source components. In: Seventh International Conference on Quality Software (QSIC 2007), pp. 316–321. IEEE (2007)

9. Kalliamvakou, E., Gousios, G., Blincoe, K., Singer, L., German, D.M., Damian, D.: The promises and perils of mining GitHub. In: Proceedings of the 11th Working Conference on Mining Software Repositories, pp. 92–101 (2014)

10. Kilamo, T., Lenarduzzi, V., Ahoniemi, T., Jaaksi, A., Rahikkala, J., Mikkonen, T.: How the cathedral embraced the bazaar, and the bazaar became a cathedral. In: Ivanov, V., Kruglov, A., Masyagin, S., Sillitti, A., Succi, G. (eds.) OSS 2020. IAICT, vol. 582, pp. 141–147. Springer, Cham (2020). https://doi.org/10.1007/978-3-030-47240-5_14

11. Lenarduzzi, V.: Towards a marketing strategy for open source software. In: Proceedings of the 12th International Conference on Product Focused Software Development and Process Improvement, Profes 2011, pp. 31–33. Association for Computing Machinery, New York (2011). https://doi.org/10.1145/2181101.2181109

12. Lenarduzzi, V., Taibi, D., Tosi, D., Lavazza, L., Morasca, S.: Open source software evaluation, selection, and adoption: a systematic literature review. In: 2020 46th Euromicro Conference on Software Engineering and Advanced Applications (SEAA), pp. 437–444 (2020). https://doi.org/10.1109/SEAA51224.2020.00076

13. Lenarduzzi, V., Tosi, D., Lavazza, L., Morasca, S.: Why do developers adopt open source software? Past, present and future. In: Bordeleau, F., Sillitti, A., Meirelles, P., Lenarduzzi, V. (eds.) Open Source Systems. OSS 2019. IFIP Advances in Information and Communication Technology, vol. 556, pp. 104–115. Springer, Cham (2019). https://doi.org/10.1007/978-3-030-20883-7_10

14. Li, X., Moreschini, S., Zhang, Z., Taibi, D.: Exploring factors and measures to select open source software. Arxiv (2021)

15. Lima, A., Rossi, L., Musolesi, M.: Coding together at scale: Github as a collaborative social network. In: Proceedings of the International AAAI Conference on Web and Social Media, vol. 8 (2014)

16. Morasca, S., Taibi, D., Tosi, D.: T-DOC: a tool for the automatic generation of testing documentation for OSS products. In: Ågerfalk, P., Boldyreff, C., González-Barahona, J.M., Madey, G.R., Noll, J. (eds.) OSS 2010. IAICT, vol. 319, pp. 200–213. Springer, Heidelberg (2010). https://doi.org/10.1007/978-3-642-13244-5_16

17. Munaiah, N., Kroh, S., Cabrey, C., Nagappan, M.: Curating GitHub for engineered software projects. Empirical Softw. Eng. 22(6), 3219–3253 (2017). https://doi.org/10.1007/s10664-017-9512-6

18. Origin, A.: Method for qualification and selection of open source software (QSOS). http://www.qsos.org. Accessed 22 Jan 2021

19. Samoladas, I., Gousios, G., Spinellis, D., Stamelos, I.: The SQO-OSS quality model: measurement based open source software evaluation. In: Russo, B., Damiani, E., Hissam, S., Lundell, B., Succi, G. (eds.) OSS 2008. ITIFIP, vol. 275, pp. 237–248. Springer, Boston, MA (2008). https://doi.org/10.1007/978-0-387-09684-1_19

20. Sbai, N., Lenarduzzi, V., Taibi, D., Sassi, S.B., Ghezala, H.H.B.: Exploring information from OSS repositories and platforms to support OSS selection decisions. Inf. Softw. Technol. **104**, 104–108 (2018). https://doi.org/10.1016/j.infsof.2018.07.009, https://www.sciencedirect.com/science/article/pii/S0950584918301526

21. Taibi, D., Lavazza, L., Morasca, S.: OpenBQR: a framework for the assessment of OSS. In: Feller, J., Fitzgerald, B., Scacchi, W., Sillitti, A. (eds.) OSS 2007. ITIFIP, vol. 234, pp. 173–186. Springer, Boston, MA (2007). https://doi.org/10.1007/978-0-387-72486-7_14

22. Tsay, J., Dabbish, L., Herbsleb, J.: Influence of social and technical factors for evaluating contribution in GitHub. In: Proceedings of the 36th international conference on Software engineering, pp. 356–366 (2014)

23. Wasserman, A.I., Guo, X., McMillian, B., Qian, K., Wei, M.-Y., Xu, Q.: OSSpal: finding and evaluating open source software. In: Balaguer, F., Di Cosmo, R., Garrido, A., Kon, F., Robles, G., Zacchiroli, S. (eds.) OSS 2017. IAICT, vol. 496, pp. 193–203. Springer, Cham (2017). https://doi.org/10.1007/978-3-319-57735-7_18

24. Wasserman, A.I., Pal, M., Chan, C.: The business readiness rating: a framework for evaluating open source technical report (2006)

OSS Scripting System for Game Development in Rust

Pablo Diego Silva da Silva, Rodrigo Oliveira Campos, and Carla Rocha[✉]

University of Brasília (UnB), Brasília, Brazil
caguiar@unb.br

Abstract. Software development for electronic games has remarkable performance and portability requirements, and the system and low-level languages usually provide those. This ecosystem became homogeneous at commercial levels around C and C++, both for open source or proprietary solutions. However, innovations brought other possibilities that are still growing in this area, including Rust and other system languages. Rust has low-level language properties and modern security guarantees in access to memory, concurrency, dependency management, and portability. The Open Source game engine Amethyst has become a reference solution for game development in Rust, has a large and active community, and endeavors in being an alternative to current solutions. Amethyst brings parallelism and performance optimizations, with the advantages of the Rust language. This paper presents scripting concepts that allow the game logic to be implemented in an external interpreted language. We present a scripting module called Legion Script that was implemented for the entity and component system (ECS) called Legion, part of the Amethyst organization. As a Proof-of-Concept (POC), we perform the Python code interpretation using the Rust Foreign Function Interface (FFI) with CPython. This POC added scripting capabilities to Legion. We also discuss the benefit of using the alternative strategy of developing a POC before contributing to OSS communities in emergent technologies.

Keywords: Tool paper · OSS · Rust language · Game engine ·
Scripting system · Amethyst game engine · Entity component system ·
Foreign function interface

1 Introduction

The rapid evolution of microprocessors and computer architecture has completely changed the game industry. The advance in computing power enables increasingly complex software solutions, and with that, a wide variety of digital games emerged [5].

Game engines implement general and necessary functionalities for several digital games. The goal is to reuse as much code that is not part of the game's logic and, at the same time, provide a stable architecture for the development of games. The game industry established design standards and code reuse to

© IFIP International Federation for Information Processing 2021
Published by Springer Nature Switzerland AG 2021
D. Taibi et al. (Eds.): OSS 2021, IFIP AICT 624, pp. 51–58, 2021.
https://doi.org/10.1007/978-3-030-75251-4_5

assist in the development of complex software, thus creating the so-called game engines.

One of the particular programming requirements in games is the need for performance. This performance requirement enforced popular game engines' implementation in compiled system languages, such as C and C++. They are low-level languages and have almost universal portability for any processor architecture [15]. However, C/C++ has a more significant learning curve and tools of greater complexity, in addition to common memory management problems [7,11], resources, and multi-platform compilation for games.

Game engines usually have scripting systems to accelerate the game development cycle and shorten the learning curve. The scripting system is an abstraction layer of the engine's modules, usually in a different language, to separate the game's specific logic from the complexities of the engine [14]. Most of the competitive engines in the gaming industry have a well-implemented scripting system with their characteristics. For example, Godot [3] is an open source game engine implemented in C++ and can execute scripts in C#, D, and its built-in scripting language, called GDScript [4].

The Rust programming language is an alternative for C and C++ in performance and portability. It also delivers performance, and the latest programming standards, such as robust packaging systems, dependency management, functional programming support, and more significant memory safety handling.

Amethyst is an open-source game engine in Rust, which, currently, does not have a scripting system. Therefore, it requires expertise in Rust to develop a game within its framework. In addition to the learning curve inherent in system languages, any changes to the code require its compilation, which can take a considerable amount of time in the Rust environment due to the compile-time checks. To facilitate new game developers' adhesion into the engine, the Amethyst community has expressed its intent to have a scripting system using a Request-For-Comments (RFC).

Contributing to a large and active OSS community, using emergent technologies with little technical documentation to specific problems, imposes some challenges. The Amethyst game engine has frequent architectural changes, and that is expected with new technologies, defying both contributors and maintainers to add new features, solve bugs, and leave stable versions available to users. Instead of contributing to an architecture that we know will be discontinued or contribute to architecture not yet mature, we opted to develop a Proof-of-Concept (POC). With this strategy, we could anticipate the new architecture problems and develop a functionality not yet present in the engine.

This paper presents an extensible scripting system for the Entity Component System, called Legion, used inside the Amethyst game engine. This system will serve as a driver for executing different interpreters and language scripts. The scripting system allows programmers with little or no Rust programming skills to start using a Rust-based game engine. We developed a Proof-of-Concept (POC) with support for the Python language to serve as example to other languages implementations. The project is an unprecedented work that highlights the concepts of implementing a scripting system in a Rust game engine. It defines a baseline for Legion and Amethyst contributors to continue working in scripting solutions while improving their software and features.

The rest of the paper is organized as follows. Section 2 presents the background, the necessary concepts of the Entity Component Systems developed in Rust. Most of the technical documentation necessary to implement the scripting system is diffuse in forums, blog posts, and other unstructured grey literature. In Sect. 3, we detail how we conduct this work. Finally, in Sect. 4, we present our results. The conclusions and lessons learned are in Sect. 5.

2 Background

Amethyst[1] is a data-driven open source game engine made with Rust, focused on being fast and configurable and maintained by the Amethyst Foundation. One of its main characteristics is the parallel Entity Component System (ECS) with user-friendly abstraction, which will manage, store and update game data using performance-focused strategies.

Amethyst community maintains an updated roadmap with the next steps for the project. The process for significant changes is based on Request For Comments (RFCs) [1] and seeks to provide a controlled, transparent, collaborative, and consistent addition of new features to the engine and its libraries.

Amethyst is a complex project organized in several modules. A scripting system gives external access to data and components through its Entity Component System. It creates a layer of interaction between the external data and the Amethyst game data. The other engine modules can be integrated in the future as the scripting becomes stable.

2.1 Entity Component System

A typical pattern in a game development project is the Entity Component System (ECS). It is a core in the engine, and it manages and organizes the objects inside a game during each iteration. This pattern favors the composition over inheritance by transforming functionalities into components, therefore, keeping each functionality self-contained and reusable. The game objects will be called Entities and will receive their behaviors through instances of the Components [6].

Entity Component Systems use a Struct of Arrays (SoA) to manage the entities and their components. Instead of having a heterogeneous array of entities, called an Array of Structs (AoS), on an ECS, each component type is stored separately, as seen in Fig. 1a. It increases the performance of queries and cache optimizations when iterating over game data.

One ECS implemented in Rust is called Specs Parallel ECS (Specs), which the Amethyst Foundation maintains. Specs is close to the classic design of an ECS presented above. It allows for parallel system execution, with both low

---

[1] https://github.com/amethyst.

overhead and high flexibility [10]. The user can declare `Components`, `Systems`, `Entities`, and `Resources`, all tied to a virtual world, which becomes the main game container.

Another `Rust` ECS is Legion [2]. Legion has minimal boilerplate and presents a better performance in some ECS operations due to its abstraction over the component types, called the archetype system. A unique combination of components defines an archetype, represented in Fig. 1b. Legion's archetype system stores components on tables created on-demand as new entities are inserted into the game world. It contrasts with Specs and most ECSs, with unique storage for each component. Those archetype tables create faster filtering and querying since it is done on the archetype level and not by entity iteration.

In Legion, while creating one or many entities, we need to match and find to which archetype they belong. If they do not match any of the existing Archetypes, Legion creates a new Archetype with the corresponding layout of the group of components that define the entity.

2.2 Specs X Legion

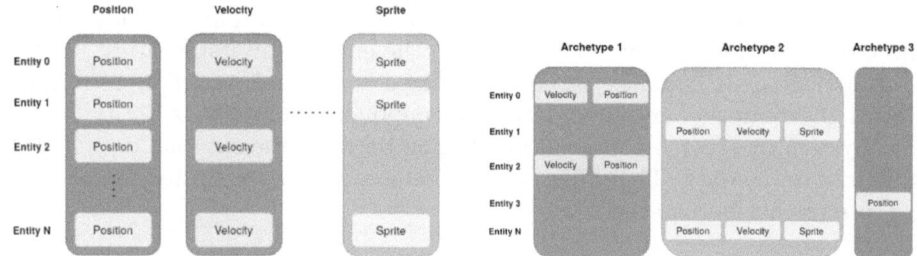

(a) Specs component data storage using arrays for each component.

(b) Legion's archetype storage for each unique component group in entities.

Fig. 1. Storage comparison between Legion and Specs.

Figure 1 illustrates the differences in data storage in both Specs and Legion, directly impacting the engine performance. Declaring data is the first step for an ECS-based game. In Specs, after declaring a component, one must register them into a `World` structure. It creates the storage table for each component and the synchronization logic for parallel access. However, Specs uses Rust's unique struct identifier, called `TypeId`, as an index to each registered component type.

A `TypeId` in `Rust` is the unique identifier for a type. It is only available for types from the program's static lifetime. Also, `Rust` does not allow runtime declarations of structs, making injecting externally defined components into Specs impracticable.

For Legion, a `Component` is defined as any type with static lifetime and implements `Rust` traits as `Sized`, `Send`, and `Sync`. The registering and storage will be done later by the ECS internal code as it combines the components to create an `Entity`. It enables building a scripting system through new components capable of sorting and uniquely identifying external components inside the Legion core.

3   Method

In this paper, we present an experience report of a contribution to a growing but still recent community of `Rust` and game engines. The use of modern technologies is also a highlight for the Amethyst engine. In this emerging technology context, we have technical challenges related to implementing a scripting system in Rust without a previous reference solution and the need to adapt and include this volatile community environment into our OSS contribution workflow.

We began with community bonding, in a traditional OSS contribution process. We got familiar with the Amethyst code base during this phase, guidelines, reading closed and open issues, forum posts, and threads focused on scripting. Amethyst has a separate repository for its Request-For-Comments (RFC), keeping discussions focused on topics such as the scripting system. They have a dedicated forum [13] for communication, questions, and discussions about the engine. Amethyst also has a Discord [12] server for faster collaborations.

Since Amethyst is a continually evolving project with many modules, we decided to adopt a Proof-of-Concept (POC) strategy. The strategy consists of developing a POC in a separate repository and implementing the minimal features necessary to validate the solution proposal. Once the community mentors review the POC, we can plan a roadmap to contribute to the Amethyst engine codebase.

In our repository, the Amethyst team could quickly review our progress and give feedback. We could do our separate version control and manage the project's risks without all the other engine modules volatile environment. The POC environment allowed us to be mentored by experienced Amethyst members. Some had participated in the scripting RFC, and some created scripting initiatives that would be incorporated into our POC. Finally, after sharing the results with the community, validating our scripting module proposal through the POC, implementing the scripting system in the Amethyst engine has fewer risks involved, and the POC serves as a guide to new contributors.

4   Results

We implemented the Proof-of-Concept during a year of research with the support of the `Rust`, Legion and Amethyst communities. It is a `Rust` module integrated into Legion. It comprises a library that adds scripting capabilities to the ECS. Our library allows running game scripts written in `Python`. As a result, it is possible to define components and entities from `Python` and still use a `Rust` ECS.

The scripting system is developed in `Rust`, `C`, and `Python`. Figure 2 depicts our architecture, using a bidirectional FFI to connect external languages to the scripting system. The developed library supports creating and querying entities from `Python` scripts stored inside Rust's domain. It does not infringe the ECS mechanisms, and it benefits from Legion. We implement a `Python` driver for demonstration purposes, but the goal is to be extensible to any other language drivers.

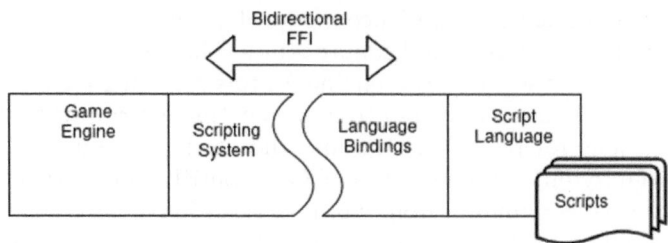

Fig. 2. Representation of the Scripting System architecture within the Amethyst Game Engine.

The `Rust` component of the scripting system is responsible for interacting with Legion and its API while also exposing this API for the `C` language driver. The language driver is written in `C`, and it is responsible for interpreting scripts and using the Rust API to inject data into Legion. Finally, in the `Python` script, the component data is appropriately defined and grouped into an entity using the `C` interpreter's API. Therefore, the game engine can directly execute our Rust code, which will execute the `C` language driver responsible for interpreting the Python script.

To build our **POC** we had to solve some problems like linking and compiling `C` code from `Rust`, calling external functions defined in `C` from `Rust`, and converting types between the two languages. Finally, we customize the **ECS** to manage external components from `Rust`. We also performed minimal modifications on Legion that still will be revised by the community.

5   Conclusion and Lessons Learned

The main result of our work is the POC called `legion_script` [8]. It is an extensible library that adds scripting capabilities to the Legion ECS. This project implements minor changes to Legion and creates another scripting layer as an API that language drivers can access. Since the implementation is on top of an ECS, The scripting system is not specific to the Amethyst game engine. Therefore, any other `Rust` project could benefit from this project.

Working in a non-consolidated area of programming, like scripting for games using `Rust`, brought some not expected challenges. These vague concepts of scripting and language interpretation generally available on the web might create the illusion that the work to be done is more straightforward than it is. It creates a scope management problem that can be entirely out of sync with the team's capabilities to produce in time. We did not find much scripting documentation for Rust since the language is relatively new. Also, smaller teams and projects tend to make decisions by word of mouth, not being recorded into repositories. Mainly, investigating and understanding decisions is much harder when documentation and working examples do not exist.

Besides the problem of scope, newly created technologies are very volatile. We expected a traditional OSS contribution process, from community bonding to pull request revision. During our planning phase, the Amethyst community never manifested any obstacles concerning Specs' use as its ECS system. However, they started migrating from Specs to Legion during our research, which directly affected our contribution relied on the ECS system. It obliged us to change our OSS contribution strategy to the development of a POC.

A lesson learned was the interaction with the community. Even though we could not find working examples of the concepts we were trying to develop, we reached out to many developers who tried approaching the problem and discussed the community's solutions. It allowed us to combine many incomplete or deprecated solutions into one working **POC**.

Besides developing documentation for scripting and Legion, our project aimed to create a platform and a runnable example. This solution can help guide the community to develop new solutions based on what we provided. Our complete work was shared through Amethyst Forums [9], Discord servers, and other social media.

References

1. Amethyst Team: Amethyst RFCS (2018). https://github.com/amethyst/rfcs. Accessed 01 Dec 2019
2. Gillen, T.: Legion (2020). https://github.com/amethyst/legion. Accessed 9 Dec 2019
3. Godot: Godot engine (2014). https://github.com/godotengine/godot. Accessed 01 Dec 2019
4. Godot: Gdscript basics (2020). https://docs.godotengine.org/en/3.2/getting_started/scripting/gdscript/gdscript_basics.html. Accessed 17 Sept 2020
5. Gregory, J.: Game engine architecture. Peters (2009)
6. Halpern, J.: Developing 2D Games with Unity: Independent Game Programming with C#. Apress (2019)
7. Novark, G., Berger, E., Zorn, B.: Plug: automatically tolerating memory leaks in c and c++ applications, January 2008
8. Oliveira, R., Silva, P.: Legion script (2020). https://github.com/redcodestudios/legion_script. Accessed 8 Oct 2019
9. da Silva, R.O.C.P.D.S.: Undergrad thesis on game scripting for legion (2020). https://community.amethyst.rs/t/undergrad-thesis-on-game-scripting-for-legion/1753. Accessed 22 Jan 2021
10. Specs: Specs parallel ECS. https://specs.amethyst.rs/docs/tutorials/ (2020). Accessed 29 Nov 2019

11. Tang, Y., Gao, Q., Qin, F.: LeakSurvivor: towards safely tolerating memory leaks for garbage-collected languages. In: USENIX Annual Technical Conference, pp. 307–320, January 2008
12. The Amethyst team: Amethyst discord (2018). https://discordapp.com/invite/amethyst. Accessed 29 Nov 2019
13. The Amethyst team: Amethyst forum (2018). https://community.amethyst.rs. Accessed 29 Nov 2019
14. Varanese, A.: Game scripting mastery. Premier Press (2003)
15. Zivkov, D., Kurtjak, D., Grumic, M.: GUI rendering engine utilizing Lua as script (2015)

Open Source Communities and Forks: A Rereading in the Light of Albert Hirschman's Writings

Robert Viseur[1](✉) and Amel Charleux[2]

[1] University of Mons, Mons, Belgium
`robert.viseur@umons.ac.be`
[2] University of Montpellier, Montpellier, France
`amel.charleux@umontpellier.fr`

Abstract. The literature dedicated to free and open source software emphasizes the support given by the community to software producers. However, the community is also a place of conflict and can sometimes experience violent splits (forks). Communities can show different forms of resistance to change. In this research, we propose a re-reading of these mechanisms of opposition in light of Albert Hirschman's theory (exit, voice, loyalty). We present the fork as a new form of defection (exit) allowed by licenses and discuss the rationality of choice for the economic actors who implement it.

Keywords: Open source · Business model innovation · Governance · Fork

1 Introduction

The literature on free and open source software emphasises the positive role of the community in the efforts of the software producer to ensure its development and popularity (Shahrivar et al. 2018). However, the literature points out the possibility of conflicts that could lead to a split in the community and, therefore, to the creation of a competing project (fork) based on the source code of the original project (Viseur 2012; Viseur and Charleux 2019). In a recent study dedicated to Claroline software, Dokeos (fork of Claroline) and Chamilo (fork of Dokeos), Charleux et al. (2019), then Viseur and Charleux (2019), note that the community is also a force of opposition resisting changes initiated by the producer in a context of business model innovation. The opposition mechanisms identified present surprising similarities with the alternative actions identified by Hirschman (2017) concerning the consumer (or citizen) faced with a declining organisation. This article therefore proposes a re-reading of the work of Charleux et al. (2019) with regard to Albert Hirschman's theory.

D. Taibi et al. (Eds.): OSS 2021, IFIP AICT 624, pp. 59–67, 2021.
https://doi.org/10.1007/978-3-030-75251-4_6

2   Community as a Source of Value

The term "free software" has been defined by the Free Software Foundation (FSF) through 4 freedoms: freedom of use, freedom of study, freedom of distribution and freedom of redistribution. The term "open source" was subsequently defined by the Open Source Initiative (OSI) on the basis of 10 criteria including in particular freedom of redistribution, access to the source code, creation of derivative works and respect for authorship. Beyond the difference in terminology, where the FSF sees free software as a political project oriented towards sharing and user emancipation, the OSI puts forward the cooperative development model as well as the associated business models and licenses (Benkeltoum 2011).

Free/open source software can arise in a variety of contexts. Firstly, it can be created by one (or more) user(s) concerned with solving a problem they encounter, in accordance with Raymond's (1999) quote: *"Every good work of software starts by scratching a developer's personal itch"*. This creation will typically take place in a professional context, as shown by the examples of Apache (Franke and Von Hippel 2003) and Claroline (Viseur and Charleux 2019). Secondly, it may be created by companies in order to pool resources and promote the dissemination of a technology or standard (Adatto 2013). Thirdly, it can be produced by a company in an entrepreneurial context with the aim of subsequently meeting customer needs. This type of open source producer is paid for by services and sometimes licences (e.g. dual licensing; cf. Välimäki 2003; Charleux and Mione 2018) while relying on a community to develop the software and disseminate the brand (Fitzgerald 2006). Examples already studied include eZ Publish (Teigland et al. 2014) and MySQL (Välimäki 2003).

3   The Community as a Brake

The community is therefore considered, for open source companies, as an important resource and a key factor in its success (Shahrivar et al. 2018). Thanks to it, the open source publisher would benefit from a reduced development cost because, on the one hand, volunteer developers would code for free and, on the other hand, users would report problems in the software (Shahrivar et al. 2018). However, the community can also be a source of disillusionment and difficulties. The commitment of developers and users is not guaranteed, either in quantity or quality. Viseur (2007) thus reports, based on 6 case studies (eZ Publish, Claroline, Exo, Plume CMS, Ekiga and Jext), that *"the most frequent contributions concern bug reports, translations and, more rarely, the addition of new functionalities"*. The hope of seeing developers coding for free is therefore put into perspective by open source project managers. Teigland et al. (2014) reveal the gap between the quality requirements of a publisher (eZ Systems) and the contributions in source code brought by the community (often in the form of extensions to the eZ Publish project). Viseur and Charleux (2019) make the same observation in the case of the Claroline project. The authors also highlight the difficult animation of the community and analyse two concrete cases of community splits (forks) (Dokeos and Chamilo). The community can therefore be a support (contributions, feedback of errors…), but also sometimes a force of resistance that can lead to new forms of competition through the forks.

The forks are motivated by several phenomena. Viseur (2012), in his analysis of the forks of 26 popular projects, isolates six motivations for forking a project: stopping the original project, technical motivations, license changes, conflict over brand ownership, problems of project governance, cultural differences and the search for new directions of innovation. Changes in business models not negotiated with the community can also lead to resistance and defection through the creation of forks (Charleux et al. 2019). The negotiation of strategic parameters such as governance appears in this context to be essential to maintain community buy-in and investment (Viseur and Charleux 2019). Alignment between the interests of project promoters and their community must be preserved to guarantee the long-term success of projects: "*effective governance and work practices that are appreciated by community members is fundamental for long-term sustainability*" (Gamalielsson and Lundell 2014). Alignment of strategy, business model and governance emerge as a necessary and difficult balance to achieve (Viseur and Charleux 2019). Markus (2007) defines open source governance as the set of means implemented for the guidance, control and coordination of fully or partially autonomous organisations and individuals on behalf of an open source development project to which they collectively contribute. It combines it with a set of characteristics including the ownership of assets (such as trademarks, licenses and copyrights), the objectives of the project, conflict resolution and rule change, and the modalities of access to tools. Viseur (2012) shows that these elements (via diverging technical choices, conflicts over brand ownership, changes in licenses, etc.) emerge as major elements of conflicts within communities that can lead to forking. The case of license changes is emblematic of these tensions that can arise between the producer and his community (Viseur and Robles 2015). License changes take place in very distinct contexts, particularly in relation to the need to adapt to the environment or change the business model. The development of cloud computing over the last ten years or so has shown how a company can move from a service delivery model to a publishing model and then to a service operator (SaaS) model by adapting the terms of its license (Viseur 2013). These changes in project parameters may alter the conditions for value creation and appropriation within the project community (Charleux and Mione 2018). If, for some, the changes can be positive and represent opportunities, for others, these changes can be harmful, leading to opposition and conflicts that can go as far as the fork.

Table 1. Gradation of opposition mechanisms (adapted from Charleux et al. 2019).

Public expression of discontent	Use of software associated with a cessation of contributions	Stopping the use of the software and migration	Fork

Conflicts within communities, however, do not always lead to forks and do not always manifest the same violence. The expression of discontent can be gradual (Charleux et al. 2019). Thus, in the particular situation of a strategic change in business model, the community may (1) publicly express its dissatisfaction, (2) continue to use the software but stop contributions, (3) stop using the software and/or (4) fork (see Table 1).

The issue of negotiation with the community in the specific context of a business model innovation (BMI) highlights the inertia brought about by the community in the face of a situation of change. This type of situation is particularly in line with the issues of equity and reversion raised in the field of open innovation by Chesbrough et al. (2018). The producer has to deal with community values and disappointment with new policies.

4   Exit and Voice (Hirschman)

In an early book originally published in 1970 ("*Exit, Voice and Loyalty. Response to Decline in Firms, Organisations and States*"), Albert Hirschman (2017) asks the questions (1) of the actions of consumers who are dissatisfied with a product or service and (2) of the means available to businesses to remedy their decline. Hirschman identifies three mechanisms used by consumers. The first is defection (exit): faced with deterioration in quality, the consumer brings competition into play. The second is voice: consumers express their dissatisfaction. The third is loyalty: the consumer resigns himself to defects through inertia, loyalty or lack of a real alternative.

Hirschman evaluates the effectiveness of these different reactions and notes in particular that defection is more or less effective in a competitive environment due to the inefficient chasing of customers. He identifies an optimum consisting of a balance between passive customers leading to the purchase of the product and vigilant customers serving as a warning signal for the company. He thus imagines that a monopoly based on the search for profits can be more effective when the speaking out allows the start of a recovery movement. As for the sacrifice of remaining loyal, it can be explained by the will to exert influence, the expectation of results (if loyalty is combined with a collective complaint), the costs of change and loyalty (judged not to be fully rational as opposed to other actions). Furthermore, Hirschman attempts in his analysis to mix economics and politics. He thus extends his analysis to non-profit organisations (e.g. political parties) and states, showing that the credibility of a threat of defection coupled with voice justifies loyalty because it gives hope for a turnaround in the organisation.

To the three mechanisms of discontent identified by Hirschman (2017), Bajoit (1988) proposes a fourth: apathy. In this schema, the dissatisfied individual can either leave (exit) or stay. If he stays, he can either protest (voice) or remain. In the latter case, he can still participate actively (loyalty) or passively (apathy). Apathy is characterised by resignation and is a form of mistrust. It does not lead to conflict and maintains social control. It plays a moderating role in the mechanisms described by Hirschman by preventing the collapse of the organisation following the flight of its members.

5   Fork as a New Form of Exit

5.1   Opposition Mechanisms and Hirschman's Model

In his work, Hirschman attempts to reconcile the economic (favouring exit) and political (favouring voice) spheres. However, free and open source software covers both spheres. Free software, which appeared in the 1980s, develops a political and ethical project of user emancipation, whereas open source places greater emphasis on the industrial and economic dimensions (Benkeltoum 2011; Fitzgerald 2006; Charleux and Mione 2018). These two conceptions coexist within communities. Moreover, the management of an open source project has in practice a political side (governance) and an economic side (business model), while the rationality of the actors is complemented by a strong moral dimension (cf. Hirschman's normative utilitarianism). Charleux et al. (2019) identify several gradations among the mechanisms of community resistance (cf. Table 1). Compared to Hirschman (cf. Fig. 1), the first (public expression of discontent) corresponds to a form of voice, while the third (migration) and the fourth (fork) constitute a form of exit. As for passive use, it is a form of loyalty but can be compared to apathy (Bajoit 1988), allowing a reasonably stable user base to be maintained. In practice, the community provides the producer with continuous feedback on its choices, and also elements likely to influence them (if the producer listens to them!), sometimes in opposition to the opinion of internal teams (Teigland et al. 2014).

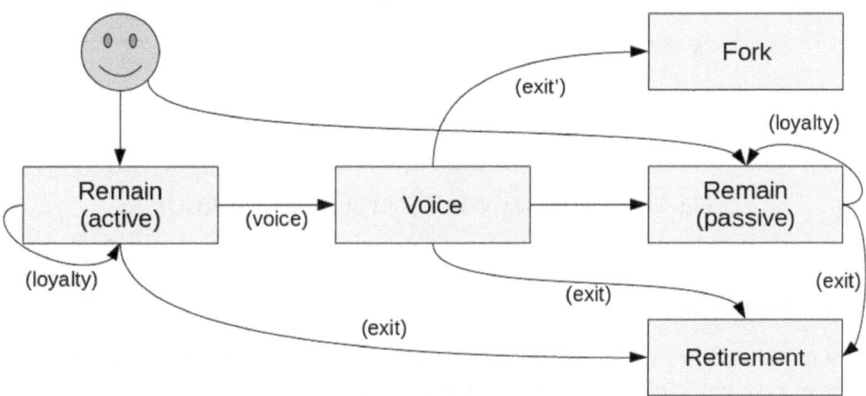

Fig. 1. Opposition mechanisms.

5.2 Extension to Open Hardware

Fauchart et al. (2017) provide material for understanding these opposition mechanisms in open hardware. The authors have mainly studied Makerbot, a company active in desktop 3D printers. Its products were initially developed in an open manner, before the development process (*"open realease' but 'closed development'"*) and then the products themselves were gradually closed, a relatively common strategy when technological uncertainty tends to be reduced and the innovative company seeks to protect itself from possible imitators (Fauchart et al. 2017; Osterloh and Rota 2007). The expression of discontent has developed as a result of various events: the gradual closure of the project, a fundraising campaign, the discovery of the conditions of use relating to intellectual property on the Thingiverse platform (also launched by Makerbot) and the filing of patents. The community has therefore reacted to various forms of misappropriations that do not necessarily violate the project's license but are at odds with the commonly accepted culture and norms (if not explicit). The misappropriations took different forms: posting on influential blogs (voice), stopping contributions (apathy), refusing to buy the product again (exit), criticising the brand (voice) and calling for a boycott (i.e. a combination of voice and exit). The company experienced a significant commercial decline as a result of these events, but also the deterioration in the quality of the machines.

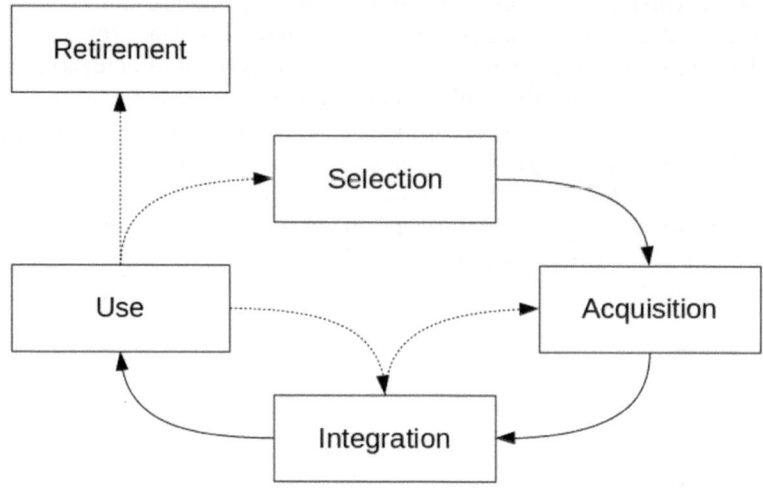

Fig. 2. The elements of Total Cost of Ownership (TCO).

5.3 Justification of Apathy

The intangible nature of the software should not lead one to believe that the cost of change is systematically low. Shaikh and Cornford (2011) thus show that the Total Cost of Ownership of software relates to a set of operations (cf. Fig. 2) including the exploration of possible alternatives, the acquisition of the chosen solution, its integration into work procedures, its use and, if the decision is taken to no longer capitalise on the same software, the exit from the solution (with a view to migration to another solution). On the one hand, the user of software within an organisation does not generally have the freedom to choose the software he uses. On the other hand, the company itself has limited degree of freedom. Thus, exploration does not require development skills, but rather the ability to define needs and evaluate offers, i.e. skills that lay users do not have (Kogut and Metiu 2001). Moreover, companies generally have to deal with legacy systems and technological integration efforts, which can be likened to a form of path dependency. The desire to migrate is curbed by the increasing returns on adoption (Foray 2002) as well as by vendor lock-in processes (Zhu and Zhou 2012) which increase the cost of defection (migration). Apathy is therefore hardly surprising even if history also contains rare examples to the contrary (e.g. PHP Nuke and its numerous forks).

5.4 Rationality of a Fork

The fork appears to be a widespread source of fear in the open source industry (Viseur 2012) even if, for others, it emerges as a form of invisible hand contributing to the sustainability of projects (Nyman et al. 2012). Nyman et al. (2012) thus insist on the fact that the very existence of this possibility of a fork stimulates the listening and consideration given by project leaders to community contributors. In this sense, the threat of a fork is seen as a factor of community recovery when its management leaves something to be desired. However, it assumes that the conflict lasts long enough, as Hirschman predicts, to allow for recovery. While this is often the case, whether the fork occurs (e.g. LibreOffice.org) or not (e.g. Java) in the end, the conflict can also too quickly lead to a fork (e.g. Dokeos), without the original project having time to adjust its governance, eventually leading to the death of the original project. While the fork may be initiated, sometimes suddenly, by a single individual (e.g. Dokeos), it is also more often the result of prior negotiation and coordination between influential project members (e.g. Chamilo) (Viseur and Charleux 2019). From the user's point of view, however, the fork facilitates defection because it lowers migration costs.

In order to better understand the economic rationality behind a fork, we propose to deepen the understanding of forks initiated (or supported) by commercial companies. For the latter, the software can be a key resource when it enables them to gain a competitive advantage on a market (e.g. dissemination of a standard through an open source implementation; Adatto 2013) or when its rate of evolution is rapid (cumulative aspect). In the latter case, the value created is more a "*value in exchange*" than a "*value in use*" (Chesbrough et al. 2018), resulting in a continuous flow of contributions that the company must be able to absorb. The company can then seek to gain control over the project through leadership (e.g., sponsoring or recruiting influential members) or by deploying resources (e.g., development capabilities) (Schaarschmidt et al. 2015). When both of these options fail, the fork can be an effective means of parallel takeover. By creating a project that competes with the initial project, the company can achieve its strategic objectives by benefiting from the impetus of the initial project. This is how Google, through the fork of the WebKit project (rendering engine), itself forked with KHTML by Apple, was able to develop and deploy its own project called Blink, a Chromium component used as a basis for several browsers (including Google Chrome). The fork provided Google with a solid foundation to develop its own rendering engine project. On the one hand, Google wanted to be able to make modifications to WebKit on a larger scale to meet different needs from those of the WebKit project (Baysal et al. 2015). The fork therefore saves on transaction costs. On the other hand, control of this technology provides the company with a strategic instrument to influence web standards (e.g. HTML5; cf. Fukami 2016) and more closely control access to the web pages on which its advertising platform business model depends (Osterwalder and Pigneur 2011; Srnicek 2018).

6   Conclusion

This research enabled us to propose a synthesis on the motivations behind the forks. Based on Charleux et al. (2019), exploiting the field offered by the Claroline, Dokeos (fork of Claroline) and Chamilo (fork of Dokeos) projects, we presented the opposition mechanisms mobilised by open source communities. We then showed the similarity between these mechanisms of opposition and the mechanisms of expression of discontent, i.e. exit, voice and loyalty, proposed by Albert Hirschman (1970, 2017) to explain the behaviour of an agent faced with the decline of an organisation. More specifically, we analysed the fork reaction as an additional manifestation to be counted as an action of exit. Drawing on Fauchart et al. (2017), which offers rich material on conflicts in the Makerbot community, we also showed the applicability of this analytical framework to an open hardware project.

This research represents a first step towards understanding open source communities in the light of Albert Hirschman's writings and contributes to an effort to theorise the mechanisms of opposition within communities. Two in-depth studies seem to us particularly worthy of interest. On the one hand, the levels of expertise and commitment of the members of an open source community (see Crowston and Howison 2005) could be distinguished in order to differentiate the opposition mechanisms implemented and discuss their dangerousness for the short-term stability of the project. On the other hand, these opposition mechanisms could be associated with indicators that can be calculated in an automated manner and thus allow for an anticipation of the most dangerous community reactions (e.g. call for boycott and fork).

Acknowledgements. This research was supported by the European Regional Development Fund as part of the FabricAr3v cross-border project.

References

Adatto, T.: Standards ouverts et implémentations FLOSS (Free Libre Open Source Software) : vers un nouveau modèle synergique de standardisation promu par l'industrie du logiciel. Terminal: Technologie de l'Information, Culture, Société, (113–114), 137–170 (2013)

Bajoit, G.: Exit, voice, loyalty... and apathy. Les réactions individuelles au mécontentement. Revue française de soc. **29–2**, 325–345 (1988)

Baysal, O., Kononenko, O., Holmes, R., Godfrey, M.W.: Investigating technical and non-technical factors influencing modern code review. Empirical Softw. Eng. **21**(3), 932–959 (2015). https://doi.org/10.1007/s10664-015-9366-8

Benkeltoum, N.: Regards sur les stratégies de détournement dans l'industrie open source. Vie sciences de l'entreprise **187**(1), 72–94 (2011)

Charleux, A., Viseur, R., Mione, A.: Open source innovation: enabler or hinderer of business model dynamics. In: Actes de XXVIIe Conférence Internationale de Management Stratégique (AIMS) (2019)

Chesbrough, H., Lettl, C., Ritter, T.: Value creation and value capture in open innovation. J. Prod. Innov. Manage. **35**(6), 930–938 (2018)

Crowston, K., Howison, J.: The social structure of free and open source software development. First Monday **10**(2) (2005)

Fitzgerald, B.: The transformation of open source software. MIS Q **30**, 587–598 (2006)

Fauchart, E., Rayna, T., Striukova, L.: Is selling caring? Norms regulating commercialisation and sharing behaviour with the open hardware RepRap. In: Proceedings of the "XXVIème Conférence Internationale de Management Stratégique" (AIMS), Lyon, France (2017)

Foray, D.: Innovation et concurrence dans les industries de réseau. Revue française de gestion **3**, 131–154 (2002)

Franke, N., Von Hippel, E.: Satisfying heterogeneous user needs via innovation toolkits: the case of Apache security software. Res. Policy **32**(7), 1199–1215 (2003)

Fukami, Y.: Open architectural competition strategy: Google's approach to innovation through standardization. In IWSECO@ICIS, pp. 80–94 (2016)

Gamalielsson, J., Lundell, B.: Sustainability of open source software communities beyond a fork: how and why has the LibreOffice project evolved? J. Syst. Softw. **89**, 128–145 (2014)

Hirschman, A. O.: Exit, Voice, Loyalty. Defection et prise de parole. Éditions de l'Université libre de Bruxelles (2017). ISBN: 978-2-8004-1625-0

Hirschman, A.O.: Exit, Voice, and Loyalty: Responses to Decline in Firms, Organizations, and States. Harvard University Press, Cambridge (1970)

Kogut, B.M., Metiu, A.: Open source software development and distributed innovation. Oxford Rev. Econ. Policy **17**(2), 248–264 (2001)

Mäenpää, H., Munezero, M., Fagerholm, F., Mikkonen, T.: The many hats and the broken binoculars: state of the practice in developer community management. In: Proceedings of the 13th International Symposium on Open Collaboration, pp. 1–9 (2017)

Markus, M.L.: The governance of free/open source software projects: monolithic, multidimensional, or configurational? J. Manage. Governance **11**(2), 151–163 (2007)

Nyman, L., Mikkonen, T., Lindman, J., Fougère, M.: Perspectives on code forking and sustainability in open source software. In: IFIP International Conference on Open Source Systems, pp. 274–279. Springer, Heidelberg (2012)

Osterloh, M., Rota, S.: Open source software development—Just another case of collective invention? Res. Policy **36**(2), 157–171 (2007)

Osterwalder, A., Pigneur, Y.: Business model nouvelle génération: Un guide pour visionnaires, révolutionnaires et challengers, vol. 1. Pearson (2011)

Raymond, E.: The cathedral and the bazaar. Knowl. Technol. Policy **12**(3), 23–49 (1999)

Schaarschmidt, M., Walsh, G., von Kortzfleisch, H.F.: How do firms influence open source software communities? A framework and empirical analysis of different governance modes. Inf. Organ. **25**(2), 99–114 (2015)

Shahrivar, S., Elahi, S., Hassanzadeh, A., Montazer, G.: A business model for commercial open source software: a systematic literature review. Inf. Softw. Technol. **103**, 202–214 (2018)

Shaikh, M., Cornford, T.: Total cost of ownership of open source software: a report for the UK. Cabinet Office supported by OpenForum europe (2011)

Srnicek, N.: Capitalisme de plateforme. L'hégémonie de l'économie numérique, Lux (2018)

Teigland, R., Di Gangi, P.M., Flåten, B.T., Giovacchini, E., Pastorino, N.: Balancing on a tightrope: managing the boundaries of a firm-sponsored OSS community and its impact on innovation and absorptive capacity. Inf. Organ. **24**(1), 25–47 (2014)

Välimäki, M.: Dual licensing in open source software industry. Syst. Inf. Manage. **8**(1), 63–75 (2003)

Viseur, R., Charleux, A.: Changement de gouvernance et communautés open source: Le cas du logiciel Claroline. Innovations **1**, 71–104 (2019)

Viseur, R., Robles, G.: First results about motivation and impact of license changes in open source projects. In: IFIP International Conference on Open Source Systems, pp. 137–145. Springer, Cham (2015)

Viseur, R.: Evolution des stratégies et modèles d'affaires des éditeurs open source face au cloud computing. Terminal. Technol. l'inf. Cult. Soc. **113–114**, 173–193 (2013)

Viseur, R.: Forks impacts and motivations in free and open source projects. Int. J. Adv. Comput. Sci. Appl. **3**(2), 117–122 (2012)

Viseur, R.: Gestion de communautés Open Source. In: 12ème Conférence de l'Association Information et Management. Lausanne (Suisse) (2007)

Zhu, K.X., Zhou, Z.Z.: Research note—lock-in strategy in software competition: open-source software vs. proprietary software. Inf. Syst. Res. **23**(2), 536–545 (2012)

Software Change Prediction with Homogeneous Ensemble Learners on Large Scale Open-Source Systems

Megha Khanna[✉], Srishti Priya, and Diksha Mehra

Sri Guru Gobind Singh College of Commerce, University of Delhi, Delhi, India
{shrishtipriya.18,dikshamehra.18}@sggscc.ac.in

Abstract. Customizability, extensive community support and ease of availability have led to the popularity of Open-Source Software (OSS) systems. However, maintenance of these systems is a challenge especially as they become considerably large and complex with time. One possible method of ensuring effective quality in large scale OSS is the adoption of software change prediction models. These models aid in identifying change-prone parts in the early stages of software development, which can then be effectively managed by software practitioners. This study extensively evaluates eight Homogeneous Ensemble Learners (HEL) for developing software change prediction models on five large scale OSS datasets. HEL, which integrate the outputs of several learners of the same type are known to generate improved results than other non-ensemble classifiers. The study also statistically compares the results of the models developed by HEL with ten non-ensemble classifiers. We further assess the change in performance of HEL for developing software change prediction models by substituting their default base learners with other classifiers. The results of the study support the use of HEL for developing software change prediction models and indicate Random Forest as the best HEL for the purpose.

Keywords: Empirical validation · Ensemble learners · Large-scale OSS · Software change prediction

1 Introduction

OSS follows the principle of open exchange and community-oriented development. These systems are in continuous development adhering to the dynamic requirements of the users [1]. Regular modifications and capability upgrades of these systems add to their complexity and size. In such a scenario, it is critical to continuously monitor and maintain these systems effectively, so that their quality does not degrade with time. Management and maintenance of these software systems require resources like time, effort and cost. However, considering the limited availability of these resources, they need to be used judiciously. One of the effective methods for sensible use of resources and guaranteeing effective software quality is the prediction of change-prone parts in

© IFIP International Federation for Information Processing 2021
Published by Springer Nature Switzerland AG 2021
D. Taibi et al. (Eds.): OSS 2021, IFIP AICT 624, pp. 68–86, 2021.
https://doi.org/10.1007/978-3-030-75251-4_7

OSS. In the event that we can predict the parts which are more inclined to changes, they can be examined thoroughly. These parts may be redesigned appropriately or rigorously verified to ensure good quality software. Therefore, constraint resources may be directed to these change-prone parts as they are likely to change because of fault correction or additional functionality requested by the users [2]. Thus, software change prediction (SCP) aids timely delivery and cost-effective management of software systems.

In recent years, various learning techniques have been assessed for SCP. Many studies have predicted the change-prone classes of software systems using statistical methods [3] and machine-learning (ML) techniques [2, 4, 5]. A recent review by Malhotra and Khanna [1] on SCP ascertained that models developed by ensemble learners exhibit better performance as compared to models developed using classifiers of other categories. Ensemble learners aggregate the output of various base learners to give an effective prediction model. They are further classified into HEL and heterogeneous ensemble learners [6]. In HEL, the same base learner is used for developing several models. However, the diversity is ensured by using varied datasets for training (for example, Bagging). On the other hand, in heterogeneous ensembles, different base learners are used to develop models using the same training dataset. The model outputs the combined outcome of base models through voting or stacking. As compared to heterogeneous ensembles, HEL can employ a larger number of base models. For instance, Random Forest (an HEL) can easily aggregate 100 decision trees developed on variants of training sets, but it is difficult to build 100 base models using diverse algorithms for aggregation using voting or stacking. Thus, this study investigates the effectiveness of SCP models developed using HEL.

We investigate the performance of eight HEL for developing SCP models on datasets obtained from five large-scale OSS. The HEL investigated were AdaBoost (AB), Bagging (BG), Dagging (DG), Decorate (DC), MultiBoostAB (MB), Random Forest (RF), Random SubSpace (RSS) and Rotation Forest (ROF). The models were developed using ten-fold cross validation and inter-version validation. We also statistically compare the effectiveness of SCP models developed using HEL with models developed using classifiers that belong to other categories such as decision tree, Bayesian learners etc. The study also analyses the change in performance of the HEL when their default base learners are replaced. The following research questions are explored in this study:

RQ1: What is the performance of SCP models developed with HEL using ten-fold cross validation?

SCP models were developed using HEL and the performance of the models was assessed using Area Under the Receiver Operating Characteristics Curve (AUC), F-measure (F1-score) and Mathew's Correlation Coefficient (MCC). The models were ranked in accordance with their performance using Friedman test. A post-hoc Wilcoxon test with Bonferroni correction was also conducted.

RQ2: What is the comparative performance of SCP models developed using HEL in RQ1 with non-ensemble learners?

We compare the performance of top 3 HEL performers (obtained in RQ1) with ten learners that belong to other categories (Classification and Regression Trees (CART), Instance-based learner (IB), J48, JRip, Logistic Regression (LR), Multilayer Perceptron

(MLP), Naive Bayes (NB), OneR, Sequential Minimal Optimization (SMO) and Voting Feature Intervals (VFI)) for developing the SCP models (ten-fold cross validation). We refer to these algorithms as non-ensemble learners. The comparison is statistically performed by analyzing AUC, F1-score and MCC measures.

RQ3: What is the performance of SCP models developed with HEL using inter-version validation? Are these SCP models better than inter-version models developed using non-ensemble learners?

The question evaluates the effectiveness of HEL for developing SCP models using inter-version validation. Thereafter, the performance of the developed SCP models is statistically ranked using the Friedman test. We also statistically compare the pair-wise difference (Wilcoxon test) in the performance of SCP models developed by the investigated HEL and those developed using the ten non-ensemble learners over three performance measures (AUC, F1-score and MCC) using inter-version validation.

RQ4: Does the change in base learners significantly improve the performance of models developed by HEL?

The question ascertains if there is any change in performance of SCP models developed using HEL when their default base learners are modified. For seven of HEL's investigated in the study (except RF), we developed SCP models (ten-fold cross validation) by replacing their base learners with ten classifiers. The classifiers evaluated as base learners were the non-ensemble learners investigated in RQ2. We statistically rank the performances (using AUC, F1-score & MCC) of different base learners for each HEL using the Friedman test. The top three base learners that attained the highest ranks were then compared with the default base learners of the HEL using Wilcoxon test.

The results of the study confirm the efficacy of HEL in the domain of SCP. The developed models can be used by software practitioners for effective management of software resources by focusing them on the problematic change-prone classes. The organization of the paper includes a broad discussion of the related literature studies in Sect. 2. Section 3 includes the various variables used in the research, the data collection procedure, performance measures and statistical tests. Section 4 provides an overview of the HEL and non-ensemble classifiers analyzed. Section 5 and 6 elaborates on the results of the study and the threats to validity respectively. Section 7 discusses the conclusions drawn and prospective future work.

2   Related Work

Various studies in the domain of software quality predictive modeling have ascertained the superiority of ensemble learners as compared to other non-ensemble algorithms [2, 4, 11]. The characteristics of some of the prominent literature studies of SCP and Software Fault Prediction (SFP), which is a related area of SCP have been listed in Table 1. The table enlists the total number of datasets used for validation and specifies the percentage of large datasets among them (in brackets). It also lists the HEL investigated, statistical test used, whether the study has evaluated different base learners, domain and the performance measure used in each study.

Table 1. Characteristics of literature studies

Study name	No. of dataset (% of large)	Name of HEL used	Statistical test used	Evaluation of different base learners	Domain (SCP/SFP)	Performance measures used
Malhotra and Khanna [2]	6 (0%)	RF, AB, LB, BG	Friedman & Wilcoxon	No	SCP	Precision, Recall, AUC, Accuracy, Balance & G-mean
Catolino and Ferruci [4]	8 (12%)	AB, RF, BG	Wilcoxon	No	SCP	Precision & Recall
Zhu et al. [5]	8 (25%)	BG	Scott-knott	Yes	SCP	Recall, F1-score, MCC & AUC
Rathore [6]	28 (35%)	DG, DC, MB, AB, ROF, ES, GR	Friedman & Wilcoxon	Yes	SFP	Precision, Recall, AUC, Specificity, G-mean1 & Gmean2
Aljamaan and Alazba [7]	11 (54%)	RF, ET, AB, GB, HG, XGB, CB	Wilcoxon	No	SFP	Accuracy & AUC
Yucular [8]	15 (20%)	AB, LB, MB, BG, RF, DG, ROF	–	Yes	SFP	AUC & F1-score
Kaur and Kaur [9]	9 (0%)	BG, BOOSTING, RF	Wilcoxon	Yes	SFP	AUC
Malhotra and Bansal [10]	11 (100%)	BG, RF, LB, AB	Friedman	No	SCP	AUC, G-mean & Balance

AB- AdaBoost, **BG-** Bagging, **CB-** CatBoost, **DC-** Decorate, **DG-** Dagging, **ES-** Ensemble Selection, **ET-** Extra Trees, **GB-** Gradient Boosting, **GR-** Grading, **HG-** Hist Gradient Boosting, **LB-** Logit Boost, **MB-** MultiBoostAB, **RF-** Random Forest, **ROF-** Rotation Forest, **XGB-** XGBoost

Ensemble learners have proven to be effective for yielding not only improved SFP models but also SCP models. In this context, Catolino and Ferrucci [4], Malhotra and Khanna [2], Malhotra and Bansal [10] assessed the performance of HEL for SCP. As depicted in Table 1, Rathore and Kumar [6], Yucular [8], Kaur and Kaur [9] have also evaluated the effect of change in base learners of HEL while developing SFP models.

However, only Zhu et al. [5] assessed the performance of HEL for SCP, by changing the underlying base learners. Kumar et al. [12] evaluated the SCP models using heterogeneous ensemble learners. The study by Aljamaan and Alazba [7] validated tree-based HEL for SFP, advocating the use of these techniques in the domain. Amongst the studies listed in Table 1, only a few percentage of the total datasets that were evaluated by the researchers were large scale OSS. To the author's best knowledge, none of the studies have examined the performance of SCP models using inter-version validation. Also, the change in base learner have been neglected in most of the SCP studies. Motivated by these research gaps, we realized that there is still a need for an extensive evaluation of HEL on large scale OSS. In the presented work, we evaluated eight HEL for SCP and also investigated the effect of change in their default base learners on their predictive capability.

3   Research Background

This section discusses the independent and the dependent variables of the study followed by the data collection procedure. It also states the performance measures and the statistical tests used in the study.

3.1   Independent Variables

Previous studies have already validated the relationship among OO metrics and change-proneness [2, 3]. For our study, we have used eleven Object Oriented (OO) metrics as the independent variables. We use the popular Chidamber and Kemerer metrics suite [13] which consists of Coupling Between Objects (CBO), Number of Children (NOC), Response For a Class (RFC), Depth of Inheritance Tree (DIT), Lack Of Cohesion in Methods (LCOM) and Weighted Methods of Class (WMC). We also used two OO metrics proposed by Lorenz and Kidd [14], i.e. Number of Instance Methods (NIM) and Number of Instance Variables (NIV). Other metrics used were Number of Private Methods (NPM) and Number of Public Methods (NPRM) of QMOOD metrics suite [7] and Lines of Code (LOC) metric. The metrics mentioned were computed using 'Understand' tool (https://www.scitools.com/).

3.2   Dependent Variable

The dependent variable ascertains the probability of change of a class in the upcoming version of the software product [2, 5]. We use the binary dependent variable with two possible values "yes" or "no", referring to whether a class changed in the newer version of the product or not.

3.3   Data Collection and Validation

In order to empirically validate our results, we collected data from five large-scale Java OSS namely- Vuze, PlantUml, LogicalDOC, Seata (Simple Extensible Autonomous

Transaction Architecture) and MPXJ. Vuze is a software used to search and download torrent files. PlantUml allows creation of UML diagrams using a simple textual description language. Seata is a distributed transaction solution that brings high performance under a microservices architecture. LogicalDOC is a document management platform. MPXJ is a file handling library for Java. Two consecutive stable versions of all these datasets were acquired from http://sourceforge.net/. The analysed versions were designated as "old" and "new" according to their release date.

These OSS were chosen based on the following criterion- (i) The common classes (data points) of each software should be 800 or more, (ii) The percentage of changed classes in "old" and "new" versions should be 20% and above, (iii) The software system should belong to varied domains like community oriented and industry oriented.

Table 2 displays the number of classes and the size (in KLOC) of the older and newer version, the common classes of both the versions (data points) and the percentage change of classes in the two versions of each dataset. As can be seen from the table, the number of classes in the investigated datasets range from 911–3616, indicating the large-size of datasets. The table also depicts the versions of datasets taken for validation while performing inter-version validation. The versions used for validation are the successive versions of those used for training.

In order to compute the dataset, at first, the OO metrics (mentioned in Sect. 3.1) were computed for the older version of each of the dataset. We use the Understand tool (https://www.scitools.com) for extracting the metrics. Secondly, the common classes of the two versions (the older version and newer version) of the dataset were compared to identify changes in the classes. Thereafter, interfaces and methods were excluded. Additionally, the metrics include various anonymous and unknown classes which were also discarded. Finally, change statistics were computed for each of the common classes in the metrics. These common classes are the data points. Change statistics include the number of inserted, deleted and modified source code lines for each data point. After computing the change statistics, we introduce a binary variable 'ALTER'. ALTER is the dependent variable of our study. For each data point, if the change statistics computed gave a non-zero positive value, the ALTER was marked as "yes", otherwise "no".

We examine the five datasets and develop models using 10-fold cross-validation and inter-version validation. In cross validation, the dataset is divided into several sub-parts, in this case ten. Then, nine of these divided datasets are used for training the model, while the remaining one is used for testing the model. This process is repeated ten times, so that each dataset part is used for testing at least once.

Inter-version validation refers to the validation of training model developed using version 'v' of a software using any of the later versions of the same software. The difference in inter-version validation is that it takes the dataset obtained from later versions of the software into account to be used as testing data rather than dividing a single dataset into training and validation data (i.e. in k-fold cross validation). For inter-version validation, we first develop an SCP model, let's say S1 using the dataset obtained from analyzing the change and metrics of version v1 & v2. Thereafter, S1 is validated using the dataset obtained from analyzing the change and metrics of version v2 & v3 (later versions of corresponding software).

Table 2. Software details

Name of software	Classes	Data points	Training data (% change)	Time gap	Size (in KLOC)	Validation data (% change)
Vuze	3590–3616	2559	5.7.4–5.7.5 (33%)	3 months	625–632	5.7.5–5.7.6 (3%)
PlantUml	2966–2772	2329	1.2020.10–1.2020.22 (31%)	7 months	265–212	1.2020.23–1.2021.1 (12%)
LogicalDOC	1948–1370	1117	8.3.4–8.4.2 (23%)	6 months	229–159	8.4.2–8.5.2 (22%)
Seata	1123–1229	906	v1.2–v1.4 (35%)	7 months	67–74	v1.4.0–v1.4.1 (5%)
MPXJ	911–942	821	8.0.0–8.2.0 (26%)	8 months	175–181	8.3.0–8.5.0 (26%)

Training data is the dataset used for ten-fold cross validation.

3.4 Performance Measures

All the models developed in the study were analyzed based on performance measures described below. The greater the value of these measures, the better is the performance of developed models. We selected these performance measures as they are robust, stable and give effective results even with imbalanced data [5, 8, 12].

- *F1-score:* It is measured as the harmonic mean of precision and recall.
- *AUC:* It is the area under the Receiver Operator Characteristic (ROC) curve. The curve is plotted for true-positive rate (y-axis) vs. false-positive rate (x-axis).
- *Mathew's Correlation Coefficient (MCC):* It is a symmetric measure which gives an unbiased result than other measures in an imbalanced data sample. The formula of MCC incorporates true positives, false positives, true negatives and false negatives. The range of MCC values lies from -1 to $+1$.

3.5 Statistical Tests

We use two non-parametric tests i.e. Friedman test and Wilcoxon signed rank test to statistically evaluate the results of our study. Friedman test is used to rank the performance of SCP models developed by HEL (in RQ1 & RQ3) on the basis of performance measure values (AUC, MCC and F1-score) across all the datasets. The test statistic is based on chi-square distribution. We further employed Wilcoxon test which is used to pairwise assess two classifiers and check if there is a significant difference in their performance. The comparison done between the two classifiers depends on the pairwise difference obtained on the values of performance measures. Bonferroni correction was used with Wilcoxon test where the chosen α value (0.05) is divided by the total number of pairwise comparisons evaluated. This correction is used to reduce the number of false positives i.e. type 1 error in statistical analysis.

4   Research Methodology

In this section, we briefly introduce the various HEL used in the study to develop SCP models. We selected these HEL as they encompass a diverse category of ensemble techniques. For instance, AB and MB are boosting classifiers, while BG and DG belong to the class of bagging learners. DC uses artificial training instances, while RSS chooses random features for model development. Lastly, ROF and RF techniques are aggregate of decision trees.

1. *AdaBoost (AB)* – It is a boosting technique that tries to improve the classification performance by training a sequence of weak learners. In this iterative technique, every following weak learner is trained to focus on the feature that was missed by the previous learner [10].
2. *Bagging (BG)* - It is a method in which the sample data is divided into independent subsets of data using bootstrap. The individual datasets are then evaluated with a weak-learner and their result is aggregated using the voting method [15].
3. *Dagging (DG)* - It is a method in which the sample data is divided into disjoint subsets (i.e. independent datasets are generated without replacement). The final result is evaluated by combining the output of weak learners on disjoint datasets using a voting scheme [6].
4. *Decorate (DC)* - This technique builds different intermediate prediction models by using specially constructed artificial training samples. The predictions from the weak learners are then integrated into one by the mean combination rule [6].
5. *MultiBoostAB (MB)* - It is an extension of AdaBoost method. It reduces the prediction bias and discrepancy in the final model by incorporating wagging techniques [16].
6. *Random Forest (RF)* - This technique consists of a number of decision trees, making sure that each one of the individual trees is distinct. Each tree is built on a subset of data points (with replacement) and the nodes of the tree use random features which are selected without replacement [17].
7. *Random SubSpace (RSS)* - It selects random subsets containing particular features of a sample dataset. The result is then predicted by the majority vote of the models created using these subsets [18].
8. *Rotation Forest (ROF)* - This method utilizes Principal Component Analysis (PCA) algorithm to choose features and data of the training sample to generate individual decision trees. The classification of each decision tree is aggregated to give the final result by the voting method [6].

Table 3 depicts the parameter settings of HEL used in this study. These are the default parameter settings of the WEKA tool.

The non-ensemble classifiers analysed in the study were- CART, IB, J48, JRip, LR, MLP, NB, OneR and SMO. These methods were chosen as they belong to different classification categories. CART and J48 belong to decision trees, NB and LR belong to statistical models, JRip and OneR belong to rule-based, IB comes under K-nearest neighbor, SMO comes under support vector machine and lastly MLP belongs to neural network. For these non-ensemble classifiers, we have used only the default parameters of the WEKA tool.

Table 3. Parameter details of HEL

HEL	Default base learners	Parameter values
AB	Decision stump	Batch Size = 100, Iterations = 10, Weight Threshold = 100
BG	REPtree	Batch Size = 100, Iterations = 10
DG	Decision stump	Batch Size = 100, Number of Folds = 10
DC	J48	Batch Size = 100, Desired Size = 15, Iterations = 50
MB	Decision stump	Batch Size = 100, Iterations = 10, Weight Threshold = 100
RF	Random tree	Batch Size = 100, Max Depth = 0, Iterations = 100
RSS	REPtree	Batch Size = 100, Iterations = 10, Sub Space Size = 0.5
ROF	J48	Batch Size = 100, Group Size = 3, Iterations = 10

5   Result Analysis and Discussion

We discuss the results of RQ's of our study in this section.

5.1   RQ1. What is the Performance of SCP Models Developed with HEL Using Ten-Fold Cross Validation?

We assess the performance of the SCP models developed using HEL by analyzing AUC, F1-score and MCC values. The models were developed using ten-fold cross validation. Figure 1 depicts a stacked graph of average performance measure values (across all the five investigated datasets).

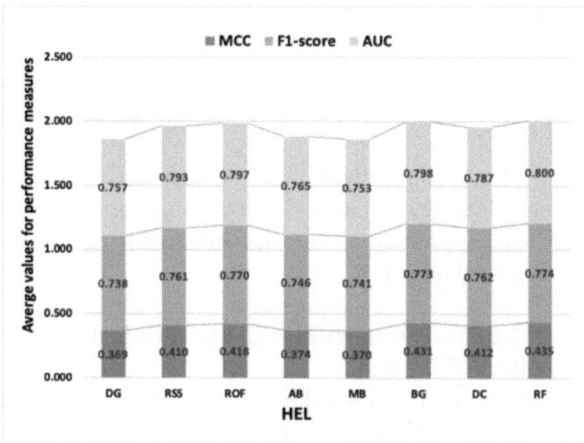

Fig. 1. Graph representing the average values of HEL for AUC, F1-score and MCC.

The AUC values of SCP models on the five datasets were in the range from 0.714–0.825, indicating their effectiveness. Similarly, F1-score values and MCC values were in the range of 0.714–0.774 and 0.370–0.435 respectively. According to the figure, the SCP models developed using RF, BG and ROF were the top 3 performers as they depicted the best average cumulative values for all the three performance measures. DG showed a decrease of 3% and 9% for average F1-score and MCC values over all datasets in comparison to the other average values obtained by HEL, thus demonstrating poor performance. Similarly, MB obtained the lowest value for AUC measure. Nevertheless, all the models developed using HEL exhibited acceptable values. These results support the use of HEL for determining change-prone classes in large OSS. We statistically analyzed the performance of the developed SCP models using the Friedman test. The test was conducted on the performance measure values (AUC, MCC and F1-score) obtained by the models on the five datasets. In all the three cases, Friedman test results were found significant at $\alpha = 0.05$. This indicates a significant difference in the performance of the investigated HEL for developing SCP models. The models developed by RF and BG ensemble classifiers obtained the best Friedman ranks using AUC, F1-score and MCC values. The next best ranks were obtained by ROF for AUC and F1-score measures and RSS for MCC measure respectively. The models developed by MB, DG and AB obtained the worst ranks.

Additionally, we employed the post-hoc Wilcoxon test with Bonferroni correction ($\alpha = 0.05$) to pairwise compare the performance of RF with other HEL (Table 4). RF outperformed (denoted by ⇑ in Table 4) all the other seven HEL, thereby, making it a desirable HEL for developing SCP models. However, its superiority was not significant.

Table 4. Wilcoxon test with Bonferroni correction of RF with all other HEL

Performance measures	AB	BG	DG	DC	MB	ROF	RSS
F1-score	⇑	⇑	⇑	⇑	⇑	⇑	⇑
AUC	⇑	⇑	⇑	⇑	⇑	⇑	⇑
MCC	⇑	⇑	⇑	⇑	⇑	⇑	⇑

⇑: better

5.2 RQ2. What is the Comparative Performance of SCP Models Developed Using HEL in RQ1 with Non-ensemble Learners?

We assess the performance of the models developed using HEL in RQ1 by comparing them with ten non-ensemble classifiers using AUC, F1-score and MCC values. Figure 2 displays the average values of the performance measures obtained by the HEL and non-ensemble classifiers across all the datasets. As depicted in figure, the models developed using the eight HEL obtained higher average values than the ten non-ensemble classifiers for AUC, F1-score and MCC values. The average AUC values for SCP models obtained by the non-ensemble classifiers on the five datasets were in the range of 0.587–0.750. Similarly, average F1-score values were in the range of 0.425–0.766 and average MCC values were in the range of 0.199–0.414. These values were lower than those reported by the models developed in RQ1. With respect to AUC, models developed by non-ensemble classifiers exhibited a 12% decrease as compared to models developed by

HEL. Similarly, F1-score values attained by the non-ensemble classifiers decreased by 7% and MCC values depicted a 15% decrement. Thus, SCP models developed using HEL show an improvement over the models developed by non-ensemble learners.

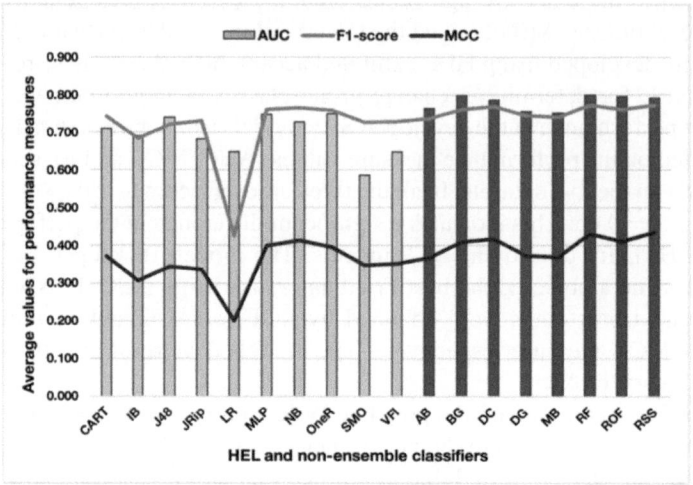

Fig. 2. Graph representing average AUC, F1-score and MCC values for HEL and non-ensemble classifiers

We also statistically evaluated the results using Wilcoxon test with Bonferroni correction at $\alpha = 0.05$ by pairwise comparing the best three performing HEL (obtained by Friedman test in RQ1) with ten non-ensemble classifiers on the three performance measures. Table 5 depicts the Wilcoxon test results and indicates that HEL perform notably better by consistently obtaining higher values than non-ensemble classifiers across all the datasets. In all the 90 pairwise comparisons performed, there was only one exception in which a non-ensemble classifier i.e. J48 obtained a higher MCC value than RSS (HEL). However, these results were not significant when Bonferroni correction was used.

5.3 RQ3. What is the Performance of SCP Models Developed with HEL Using Inter-version Validation? Are These SCP Models Better Than Inter-version Models Developed Using Non-ensemble Learners?

We assess the performance of SCP models developed using HEL and non-ensemble learners using inter-version validation by evaluating AUC, F1-score and MCC measures. Table 6 and 7 depict the average values of performance measures obtained on five datasets by HEL and non-ensemble learners respectively. The average AUC values for SCP models developed by HEL were in the range 0.727–0.764. The average values for F1-score and MCC were in the range of 0.769–0.790 and 0.160–0.255 respectively. On the other hand, the average performance measure values for non-ensemble learners were in the range 0.619–0.759 (AUC), 0.544–0.806 (F1-score) and 0.150–0.210 (MCC), which were considerably lower than those obtained by models developed using HEL.

Table 5. Comparing HEL & non-ensemble classifiers using AUC, F1-score and MCC

AUC

	MLP	SMO	NB	IB	VFI	CART	J48	JRIP	ONER	LR
RF	⇑	⇑	⇑	⇑	⇑	⇑	⇑	⇑	⇑	⇑
BG	⇑	⇑	⇑	⇑	⇑	⇑	⇑	⇑	⇑	⇑
ROF	⇑	⇑	⇑	⇑	⇑	⇑	⇑	⇑	⇑	⇑

F1-score

	MLP	SMO	NB	IB	VFI	CART	J48	JRIP	ONER	LR
RF	⇑	⇑	⇑	⇑	⇑	⇑	⇑	⇑	⇑	⇑
BG	⇑	⇑	⇑	⇑	⇑	⇑	⇑	⇑	⇑	⇑
ROF	⇑	⇑	⇑	⇑	⇑	⇑	⇑	⇑	⇑	⇑

MCC

	MLP	SMO	NB	IB	VFI	CART	J48	JRIP	ONER	LR
RF	⇑	⇑	⇑	⇑	⇑	⇑	⇑	⇑	⇑	⇑
BG	⇑	⇑	⇑	⇑	⇑	⇑	⇑	⇑	⇑	⇑
RSS	⇑	⇑	⇑	⇑	⇑	⇑	⇓	⇑	⇑	⇑

⇑: better, ⇓: worse

Table 6. Performance measure values of HEL

	AB	BG	DG	DC	MB	RF	RSS	ROF
AUC	0.727	0.756	0.732	0.764	0.729	0.759	0.758	0.749
F1-score	0.769	0.786	0.780	0.778	0.789	0.781	0.790	0.789
MCC	0.160	0.204	0.175	0.195	0.210	0.255	0.207	0.208

Table 7. Performance measure values of non-ensemble learners

	MLP	SMO	NB	IB	VFI	CART	J48	JRip	OneR	LR
AUC	0.743	0.619	0.745	0.704	0.692	0.715	0.705	0.643	0.620	0.759
F1-score	0.797	0.815	0.806	0.766	0.544	0.781	0.779	0.792	0.792	0.802
MCC	0.196	0.206	0.200	0.208	0.150	0.196	0.192	0.184	0.184	0.210

Further, in order to determine the best HEL for developing SCP models using inter-version validation, we statistically assessed their performances using Friedman test. Though the test results were not found significant for AUC measure and F1-score, the results were significant for MCC at $\alpha = 0.05$. RF, BG and RSS were the top three performers obtaining the highest values for MCC.

We further used Wilcoxon test with Bonferroni correction to validate the performance of eight HEL with the ten non-ensemble learners on MCC values. Figure 3 shows the number of non-ensemble learners that performed better (shown below the axis) and worse (shown above the axis) than HEL when validated using inter-version validation. The figure illustrates that the SCP models developed using HEL performed better than those developed using non-ensemble learners in the majority of cases (54%), however Boosting techniques (AB and MB) and DG showed poor performance measure values than most of the investigated non-ensemble learners. Similar trend was observed when Wilcoxon test was conducted using AUC and F1-score values. Wilcoxon results also depicted that the MCC values for SCP models developed using RF were the best amongst all non-ensemble learners (Fig. 3) as the models developed using RF were superior than all the other investigated non-ensemble learners.

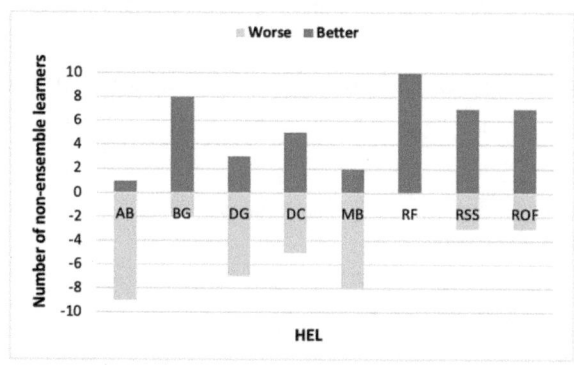

Fig. 3. Wilcoxon results for MCC values (Inter-version validation)

5.4 RQ4. Does the Change in Base Learners Significantly Improve the Performance of Models Developed by HEL?

We assess the performance of HEL by changing their default base learners for developing SCP models using ten-fold cross validation. We used the non-ensemble classifiers (used in RQ2) as the various base learners. However, it may be noted that since RF is the aggregation of multiple decision trees where each decision tree uses different features, we could not alter its base learner. For all the other seven investigated HEL, we altered the base learners to evaluate the change in their performance.

Figure 4 shows the AUC box-plots for the developed SCP models by changing the base learners of investigated HEL. The figure depicts that majority of the investigated HEL show best results for SCP models with their default base learners. It was also observed that most of the HEL show improved performances with J48, JRip and CART as their base learners in comparison to their default base learner (although, the percentage change was less than 1%). However, all the HEL with SMO and VFI as their base learners obtain the lowest values. There was an average decrease of 16% for the AUC value, 33% for the MCC value and 17% for F1-score for SMO and VFI in comparison to default base learner.

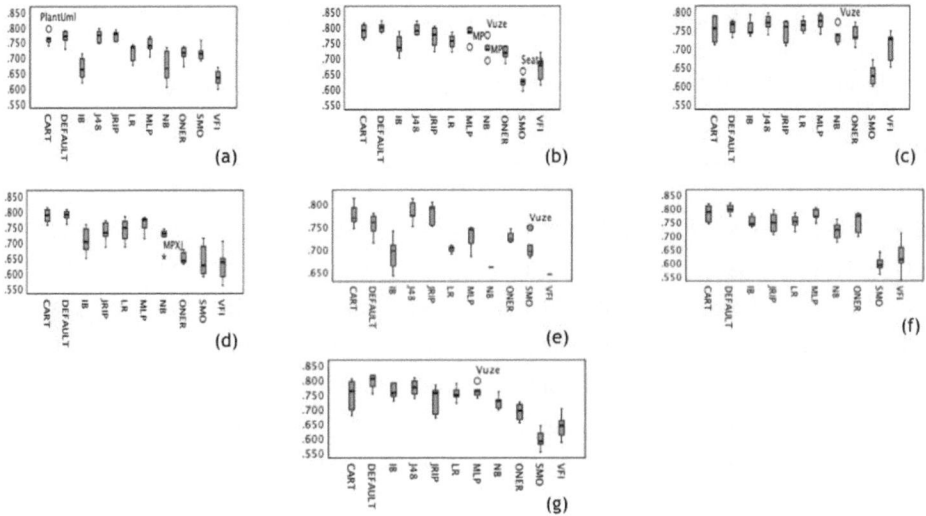

Fig. 4. AUC box plots for different base learners - (a) AB, (b) BG, (c) DG, (d) DC, (e) MB, (f) ROF, (g) RSS

To rank the performance of SCP models developed using HEL with different base learners, we performed the Friedman test. Table 8 shows the best three ranks obtained by various base learners for all the HEL on three performance measures (AUC, F1-score and MCC). For each HEL, we evaluated eleven possibilities, one with their default base learner and other ten with the rest of the base learners used in this study. The Friedman test result was found significant at $\alpha = 0.05$. According to Friedman results on AUC, F1-score and MCC values, in addition to corresponding default base learners, J48, JRip and CART were designated as the best base learners for most of the investigated HEL. The MLP technique also exhibited effective results when used as a base learner for DG and MB. On the other hand, SMO, VFI and OneR were found to be the worst base learners.

Furthermore, we used post-hoc Wilcoxon test with Bonferroni correction to validate the performance of HEL with their default base learner and the top three base learners (according to the Friedman test). The test evaluates a total of 63 pairwise comparisons of HEL with varied base learners for the three performance measures (AUC, F1-score and MCC). According to the test results, the performance of SCP models developed using HEL with different base learners showed an improvement in only 8 of the 21 cases when AUC was evaluated. AB, DG and MB progressively increased their AUC performance when their default base learners were altered. But in majority of the cases, there was a decline in the AUC performance of other HEL when their base learners were changed. Similar results were observed when Wilcoxon test was performed using F1-score and MCC values. Thus, changing the default base learner does not necessarily improve the performance of HEL for developing SCP models.

Table 8. Top ranks of base learners according to Friedman test

HEL	Friedman ranks for AUC			Friedman ranks for F1-score			Friedman ranks for MCC		
	Rank 1	Rank 2	Rank 3	Rank 1	Rank 2	Rank 3	Rank 1	Rank 2	Rank 3
AB	JRip	DFT	J48	JRip	J48	DFT	JRip	J48	CART
BG	DFT	J48	CART	DFT	J48	CART	J48	DFT	CART
DG	MLP	J48	LR	DFT	J48	MLP	MLP	J48	JRip
DC	DFT	J48	CART	DFT	CART	J48	CART	DFT	J48
MB	J48	JRip	CART	JRip	MLP	DFT	JRip	CART	MLP
ROF	DFT	J48	CART	DFT	CART	J48	DFT	CART	J48
RSS	DFT	J48	MLP	DFT	CART	IB	CART	DFT	J48

DFT: Default Base Learner

5.5 Discussion of Results

The results of the study indicate the effectiveness of the investigated HEL for developing SCP models. The performance of HEL was evaluated on AUC, F1-score and MCC for five large OSS by ten-fold cross validation and inter-version validation. For ten-fold cross validation, the mean AUC value exhibited by all the HEL across the datasets was 0.778 with a standard deviation (SD) of 0.02. Similarly, the mean F1-score and MCC values were 0.758 (SD = 0.02) and 0.402 (SD = 0.06) respectively. The values obtained by all the HEL for the three performance measures are close to the mean value, signifying that all the ensemble learners are competent and effective for developing SCP models [19, 20]. Similar results were obtained using inter-version validation for which the mean AUC and F1-score were 0.747 and 0.783 respectively. However, there was a slight decline in the MCC values obtained using inter-version validation (mean MCC = 0.202).

It was observed that the SCP model developed using RF was the most efficient as it obtained the highest values for all the investigated performance measures. The maximum values obtained by models developed using RF (ten-fold cross validation) for AUC, F1-score and MCC were 0.825, 0.796, and 0.518 respectively across all the datasets. Even for inter-version validation, the average AUC value obtained by RF exhibited a 2% increase and MCC exhibited a 31% rise compared to the other HEL. RF works on the principle of bagging using random feature selection method. Since, RF is a combination of decision trees which are developed using varied samples of the dataset (chosen randomly with replacement) and varied predictors (chosen randomly without replacement from the original set of features), it provides an edge over other HEL [21]. Also, RF can handle large amount of data and tends to decrease overfitting [17]. These characteristics of RF make it an ideal technique for developing SCP classification models.

According to Friedman test results (both ten-fold & inter-version), SCP models developed by BG, ROF and RSS also yielded effective results as they were amongst the top-3 HEL in majority of the cases. ROF technique involves the application of BG and feature selection to perform PCA which is used to build decision trees. This ensures accuracy and diversity of the individual decision trees [22]. BG tends to reduce variance as it performs sampling of data with replacement. Just as the variance decreases, overfitting also decreases which increases the accuracy of BG algorithm [23].

AB and MB (boosting techniques) and DG performed poorly in comparison to other investigated HEL. Boosting techniques (AB and MB) work on weak base learners which are sensitive to noise. Boosting techniques also give more weight to misclassified data and hence if the data contains outliers, it will tend to increase overfitting [23]. This could be a possible reason for their poor results.

The results obtained by SCP models developed using HEL on inter-version validation were comparable to the results obtained by ten-fold cross validation. For instance, in LogicalDOC the AUC and F1-score values of SCP models developed using RF (ten-fold cross validation) were 0.785 and 0.796 respectively. On the other hand, the inter-version model on LogicalDOC (using RF) exhibited an AUC and F1-score value 0.707 and 0.758 respectively. Though, there was a slight decrease (up to 10%) in these performance measure values when using inter-version, they can be considered at par with ten-fold cross validation results.

As indicated by the values of performance measures (Fig. 2), SCP models (ten-fold cross validation) developed using HEL were found to be superior to the models developed using non-ensemble classifiers. There was a decrease of 6% in the values of the non-ensemble classifier obtaining the highest value for AUC as compared to the highest value of AUC obtained by the best HEL (RF). Likewise, a decrease of 1% and 5% was observed for F1-score and MCC values respectively. Unmistakably, the higher values obtained by HEL for all performance measures highlights their accuracy and efficiency for predicting change-prone classes. Even the HEL obtaining the lowest Friedman rank (MB) secured a minimum value of 0.753 over all datasets for AUC. This value is greater than the highest value obtained by the non-ensemble learner (LR) for AUC which was 0.750. The superiority of HEL was also confirmed when the SCP models were developed by inter-version validation. There was a slight decline in the performance of SCP models developed using non-ensemble learners in comparison to those developed using HEL. On an average, there was a 7%, 2% and 4% decline for AUC, F1-score and MCC values. This signifies the effectiveness of HEL for prediction tasks. It may be noted that the common errors in a model are often described in terms of two properties- bias and the variance [23]. Ensemble techniques aim to minimize variance and bias by combining various base models to build one optimal prediction model. The reduction in the variance element of generalization error improves the prediction capacity of the models developed by ensemble learners. Therefore, the results obtained by HEL for developing SCP models are robust as HEL reduces these errors and obtains an evenly spread values for all performance measures.

As observed in the results of RQ4, when the default base learners of the proposed HEL for developing SCP models are altered, there is a relative decline in their performance. With respect to AUC, there was a drop of 2–10% in the performances of HEL across all the datasets. MB depicted the lowest decrease of 2% and the highest decrease of 10% was obtained by RSS for AUC values. F1-score and MCC values also underwent a similar decrease. Since the percentage decrease was low, we statistically ranked all the base learners investigated for a specific HEL. J48, CART, JRip and MLP were ranked as the top base learners as they gave better values for the performance measures compared to the other investigated base learners. The results from the study suggested that when these base learners are used, there was a positive effect on the AUC values for AB, MB (boosting techniques) and DG.

Amongst the top three base learners, two of the learners (J48 and CART) were decision tree algorithms. These learners use greedy approach. They split the data on the best feature by considering the accuracy of all the available features [23]. As decision trees implicitly perform feature selection they are successful as base learners for HEL. However, in order to generalize these results, we need to ascertain the use of HEL with other base learners for developing SCP models on even larger datasets. Since the performance difference of HEL with altered base learners was not significant, researchers may use the default base learners for developing SCP models.

The SCP models developed in the study can be put into use by the software industry while allocating resources like time, effort and cost. An effective way for maintenance of large OSS is the prediction of change-prone classes so that more resources may allocated to these classes. To assess the efficacy of the developed SCP models, we carried out cost-benefit analysis on all five datasets using HEL techniques [25]. The cost/benefit gain is computed as the saving of resources if the developed SCP models are put into use instead of random testing. The higher the value of cost/benefit gain, the more successful is the SCP model. The percentage cost/benefit gain given by all HEL for the five datasets was found to be in the range of 26%–54%. This indicates optimum use of constraint resources if the developed models are put into effect by software managers.

6   Threats to Validity

The SCP models developed in the study using HEL have been statistically evaluated using Friedman and Wilcoxon test. This substantiates the conclusion validity of our results. Moreover, the performance of the models were evaluated on three performance measures- AUC, F1-score and MCC. This increases the credibility of the results.

The independent variables used in the study are the commonly used metrics in software engineering literature. These variables have already been validated as predictors in earlier studies [2, 3, 9], reducing the construct validity threat in the study. The results of the study do not take into account the confounding effect of size of the projects and other characteristics in development of the SCP models. However, this was not the intent of the study.

The results of the study are validated on five large OSS belonging to varied domains. However, researchers should perform empirical validation on OSS of different sizes (small, medium, large) along with the OSS developed using different languages like Python, JavaScript, C# to enhance the generalizability of obtained results.

7   Conclusion and Future Work

The study performs an analysis of eight HEL namely - AB, BG, DG, DC, MB, RF, RSS, ROF to determine change-prone classes in five large-scale OSS (developed in Java language). SCP models were developed using ten-fold cross validation as well as inter-version validation. The effectiveness of the HEL was statistically evaluated using three performance measures - AUC, MCC and F1-score. The key results of the study are as follows-

- Each of the eight HEL analyzed in the study attained effective results for predicting change-prone classes. Particularly, RF was the best HEL as we observed an increase of 3% in AUC, 2% in F1-score and 9% in MCC values in the SCP models developed by RF using ten-fold cross validation as compared to the models developed by the other seven investigated HEL. Other HEL which showed promising results were BG, ROF and RSS.
- The results from the study indicated that SCP models (using ten-fold cross validation) developed by HEL are superior than those developed by non-ensemble classifiers. It was observed that the top three ranked HEL (RF, BG, ROF, RSS) when compared to the non-ensemble learners showed an improvement of up to 15%, 10% and 23% for AUC, F1-score and MCC values respectively.
- The outcomes of the study also showed that SCP models developed by HEL using inter-version validation methods have better performance than non-ensemble learners. HEL showed an increase of 7% in the AUC values as compared to the non-ensemble learners. In a similar manner, an increase of 2% and 5% was indicated by the HEL for F1-score and MCC values.
- The results of the study illustrate that the change in base learners for each HEL does not significantly improve their performance in the SCP domain. BG, DC, ROF and RSS showed a decline in their performance with J48, CART, JRip and MLP as their base learners. On the other hand, AB, DG and MB exhibited enhanced performances with these base learners. Thus, changing the base learners might not always give promising results for HEL, while developing SCP models.

In future, we would like to evaluate the heterogeneous ensemble classifiers for predicting change-prone classes. For the continuous growth of software, the maintenance of large and complex software systems is important. It is comprehended that efficient SCP models reduce the effort and cost required for maintaining large OSS. The results of the study would aid software managers in choosing optimum classifiers for developing SCP models. Furthermore, effective planning and resource allocation can be implemented using the developed SCP models.

References

1. Malhotra, R., Khanna, M.: Software change prediction: a systematic review and future guidelines. eInformatica Softw. Eng. J. 13(1), 227–259 (2019)
2. Malhotra, R., Khanna, M.: An empirical study for software change prediction using imbalanced data. Empirical Softw. Eng. 22(6), 2806–2851 (2017)
3. Zhou, Y., Leung, H., Xu, B.: Examining the potentially confounding effect of class size on the associations between object metrics and change-proneness. IEEE Trans. Softw. Eng. 35(5), 607–623 (2009)
4. Catolino, G., Ferrucci, F.: Ensemble techniques for software change prediction: a preliminary investigation. In: IEEE Workshop on Machine Learning Techniques for Software Quality Evaluation (MaLTeSQuE), pp. 25–30. IEEE (2018)

5. Zhu, X., He, Y., Cheng, L., Jia, X., Zhu, L.: Software change-proneness prediction through combination of bagging and resampling methods. J. Softw. Evol. Process **30**(12), 1–17 (2018)
6. Rathore, S.S., Kumar, S.: An empirical study of ensemble techniques for software fault prediction. Appl. Intell. 1–30 (2020)
7. Aljamaan, H., Alazba, A.: Software defect prediction using tree-based ensembles. In: 16th ACM International Conference on Predictive Models and Data Analytics in Software Engineering, pp. 1–10. ACM (2020)
8. Yucular, F., Ozcift, A., Boranbag, E., Kilinc, D.: Multiple-classifiers in software quality engineering: combining predictors to improve software fault prediction ability. Eng. Sci. Technol. Int. J. **23**(4), 938–950 (2020)
9. Kaur, A., Kaur, K.: Performance analysis of ensemble learning for predicting defects in open source software. In: 2014 International Conference on Advances in Computing, Communications and Informatics (ICACCI), pp. 219–225. IEEE (2014)
10. Malhotra, R., Bansal, A.: Investigation of various data analysis techniques to identify change-prone parts of an open source software. Int. J. Syst. Assurance Eng. Manage. **9**(2), 401–426 (2017)
11. Elish, M.O., Aljamaan, H., Ahmad, I.: Three empirical studies on predicting software maintainability using ensemble methods. Soft. Comput. **19**(9), 2511–2524 (2015)
12. Kumar, L., Lal, S., Goyal, A., Murthy, N.L.: Change-proneness of object-oriented software using combination of feature selection techniques and ensemble learning techniques. In: Proceedings of the 12th Innovations on Software Engineering Conference (formerly known as India Software Engineering Conference), pp. 1–11. ACM (2019)
13. Chidamber, S., Kemerer, C.: A metric suite for object-oriented design. IEEE Trans. Softw. Eng. **20**, 476–493 (1994)
14. Lorenz, M., Kidd, J.: Object-oriented Software Metrics: A Practical Guide. Prentice-Hall, Inc. (1994)
15. Breiman, L.: Bagging predictors. Mach. Learn. **24**(2), 123–140 (1996)
16. Webb, G.I.: Multiboosting: a technique for combining boosting and wagging. Mach. Learn. **40**(2), 159–196 (2000)
17. Brieman, L.: Random forests. Mach. Learn. **45**(1), 5– 32 (2001)
18. Ho, T.K.: The random subspace method for constructing decision forests. IEEE Trans. Pattern Anal. Mach. Intell. **20**(8), 832–844 (1998)
19. Chicco, D., Jurman, G.: The advantages of the Matthews correlation coefficient (MCC) over F1-score and accuracy in binary classification evaluation. BMC Genomics, **21**(1), 1–13 (2020)
20. Shatnawi, R.: Improving software fault-prediction for imbalanced data. In: 2012 International Conference on Innovations in Information Technology (IIT), pp. 54–59. IEEE, UAE (2012)
21. Baskin, I.I., Marcou, G., Horvath, D., Varnek, A.: Random subspaces and random forest. Tutorials Chemoinform. 263–269 (2017)
22. Bustamam, A., Musti, M.I.S., Hartomo, S., Aprilia, S., Tampubolon, P.P., Lestari, D.: Performance of rotation forest ensemble classifier and feature extractor in predicting protein interactions using amino acid sequences. BMC Genom. **20**(9), 950–963 (2019)
23. Alpaydin, E.: Introduction to Machine Learning, 3rd edn. MIT Press, Cambridge (2014)
24. Malhotra, R., Khanna, M.: An explanatory study for software change prediction in object-oriented systems using hybridized techniques. Autom. Softw. Eng. **24**(3), 673–717 (2017)
25. Sohail, M.N., Jiadong, R., Uba, M.M., Irshad, M., Iqbal, W., Arshad, J., John, A.V.: A hybrid forecast cost benefit classification of diabetes mellitus prevalence based on epidemiological study on real-life patient's data. Sci. Rep. **9**(1), 1–10 (2019)

Author Index